D0822517

THE
ROSWELL
LEGACY

THE

ROSWELL

LEGACY

THE UNTOLD STORY OF THE FIRST
MILITARY OFFICER AT THE 1947 CRASH SITE

JESSE MARCEL, JR., AND LINDA MARCEL

FOREWORD BY STANTON T. FRIEDMAN

AUTHOR OF FLYING SAUCERS AND SCIENCE

New Page Books
A division of The Career Press, Inc.
Franklin Lakes, NJ

THE ROSWELL LEGACY
EDITED AND TYPESET BY KARA REYNOLDS
Cover design by Ian Shimkoviak, bookdesigners.com
Printed in the U.S.A. by Book-mart Press

To order this title, please call toll-free 1-800-CAREER-1 (NJ and Canada: 201-848-0310) to order using VISA or MasterCard, or for further information on books from Career Press.

The Career Press, Inc., 3 Tice Road, PO Box 687,
Franklin Lakes, NJ 07417
www.careerpress.com
www.newpagebooks.com

Library of Congress Cataloging-in-Publication Data
Marcel, Jesse, 1938–
    The Roswell legacy : the untold story of the first military officer at the 1947 crash site / by Jesse Marcel, Jr. and Linda Marcel ; foreword by Stanton T. Friedman.
        p. cm.
    Includes index.
    ISBN 978-1-60163-026-1
    1. Unidentified flying objects—Sighting and encounters—New Mexico—
Roswell. 2. Marcel, Jess. I. Marcel, Linda. II. Title.
TL789.3.M355 2008
001.942--dc22

                                            2008027704

This book is dedicated to Jesse A. Marcel, Sr.,
Major, United States Army Air Force.

ACKNOWLEDGMENTS

The list of people to whom this book should be dedicated is most certainly longer than would fit on a few pages. For the sake of brevity, I will list those who come to mind most readily.

First and foremost, I dedicate this book to an Army Air Force officer, my greatest hero with his eyes to the skies. Dad, I have kept my promise!

My wife, Linda, has stood beside me through more than any woman should be expected to endure. She has goaded me—always lovingly—to do what we both knew I needed to do, allowed me to rant at the injustices of the world, and reassured me when I felt that life was most unfair.

To Dr. Herb Brosz—a down-to-earth Montana cowboy.

To all my kids, we've had our great times, as well as some not so great, but I think that each of you know that I've always loved you.

To my fellow men and women in arms, I cannot begin to express the pride I feel for having been so privileged as to serve with you. May you all be kept safe, and feel the honor you so greatly deserve.

To Stan Friedman, what can I say? Your unbending quest for truth has been an inspiration to me, and I am ever grateful for your support throughout the years.

To Ron Kaye and Connie Schmidt, I give my thanks for turning decades of memories into a book in which my father and I can take real pride.

And finally, to you, my readers. It is my hope that you will always seek—and find—truth, and that one day, the world will look at you and share your hunger. May your lives be filled with wonder, every day.

CONTENTS

Foreword by Stanton T. Friedman   ➤ 11

Introduction   ➤ 19

Chapter 1 ➤ The Path to Roswell   ➤ 27

Chapter 2 ➤ The Debris   ➤ 45

Chapter 3 ➤ Government Cover-Up? You Decide   ➤ 63

Chapter 4 ➤ What Was a Mogul Balloon?   ➤ 77

Chapter 5 ➤ Dr. Moore: Mogul Balloon Scientist   ➤ 85

Chapter 6 ➤ A Government Official's Admission   ➤ 95

Chapter 7 ➤ Other Visits   ➤105

Chapter 8 ➤ "Along for the Ride of My Life": Linda's Story   ➤ 115

Chapter 9 ➤ The Domino Effect   ➤ 129

Chapter 10 ➤ Life in the Cosmos: Beyond Roswell   ➤ 143

Epilogue   ➤ 167

Appendix ➤ History of the 509th   ➤ 171

Index   ➤ 175

About the Authors   ➤ 185

FOREWORD
By Stanton T. Friedman

had no idea when I first heard the name *Jesse Marcel* that 28 years later I would still be involved in the investigation of the phenomenon known as the Roswell Incident. I was at a TV station in Baton Rouge, Louisiana, in 1978, to do three different interviews to help promote my lecture "Flying Saucers ARE Real" at Louisiana

State University that evening. The first two interviews had gone off without a hitch. Unfortunately, the third reporter was nowhere to be found in those pre-cell-phone days. The station manager was giving me coffee, apologizing, looking at his watch. He knew the woman who had brought me to the station for the university, and that other activities were scheduled. We were just chatting, when, out of the blue, he said, "The person you ought to talk to is Jesse Marcel."

Being the outstanding UFO investigator and the nuclear physicist that I am, my response was really not very sharp. "Who is he?" I asked. My teeth practically fell out when he said, "Oh, he handled wreckage of one of those saucers you are interested in when he was in the military."

"What? What do you know about him? Where is he?"

"He lives over in Houma. He's a great guy. We are old ham radio buddies. You ought to talk to him!"

By this time the reporter had shown up. Fortunately the launch window had been just long enough for another UFO case to be brought up. The interview was done, and there was a great crowd that night at LSU. The next day, from the airport, I called telephone information in Houma. I had no idea where it was, other than that it was in Louisiana. There was a listing for a Jesse A. Marcel, so I called him.

I mentioned the TV station manager as a kind of reference, and then we spoke for some while. Jesse told me his story about his involvement in the recovery of strange wreckage outside Roswell, New Mexico, in company with Counter Intelligence Corps officer Sheridan "Cav" Cavitt, on orders from Colonel William Blanchard, the base commander. Jesse had been a major, the base intelligence officer. The story of what happened has since been told in numerous books, such as *The Roswell Incident* by Charles Berlitz and William L. Moore, and *Crash at Corona* by Don Berliner and myself.

Jesse noted that he had been told not to say anything, but that just after the incident occurred, his picture had appeared in newspapers all over the United States, and some overseas. The "official" explanation was that what was recovered was just a weather balloon radar reflector. But Marcel never believed that, and the notion that neither he nor Colonel Blanchard (who was later a four-star general) could not recognize such a common device was absurd.

The problem for me was that, at first, Jesse didn't remember the precise date of the incident. Yet his story was credible, and it whetted my curiosity. I knew that the summer of 1947 had been a very busy flying saucer time, beginning with the famous Kenneth Arnold sighting in June, and escalating in the next few weeks. But I really didn't have enough to go on at that point.

So, after speaking with Jesse, I filed the story in my gray basket and shared it with Bill Moore, whom I knew because we had both earlier been active in the UFO Research Institute of Pittsburgh back in the late 1960s. Bill had moved to Minnesota, and I was living in Hayward, California, and lecturing all over. A few months later, after a lecture to a packed hall that I gave at Bemidji State College in Bemidji, Minnesota, I was quietly approached, at my table of papers, by Vern and Jean Maltais, who asked if I had heard anything about a crashed saucer in New Mexico. I said I had heard something, but wanted to know more. They spoke of the experience of their friend Grady "Barney" Barnett, who had worked for the soil conservation service out of Socorro, New Mexico. Barnett had seen a crashed saucer and strange bodies, and was chased off by the military along with some college people who were also there. But the Maltaises didn't have an exact date either. I obtained phone and address contact information from them, and the next day I passed them on to Bill Moore, who was then teaching in Minnesota.

Bill found a third story about a crashed saucer in New Mexico in the English magazine, *Flying Saucer Review*. This story was about an English actor, Hughie Green, who had heard a story on the radio while driving from Los Angeles to Philadelphia. He was able to pin down the date as early July, 1947, as such trips were not very common back then. Bill went to the Periodicals Department at the University of Minnesota Library and found the story. This was a real boost, as it named other people that were involved, and validated what Jesse had said. On July 8, 1947, many evening newspapers all over the United States carried the very exciting story of a crashed saucer (sometimes called a disc) recovered by a rancher outside Roswell.

This began an intensive research effort that lasted years for Bill and me. In 1980, the first book, *The Roswell Incident* by Bill Moore and Charles Berlitz (of *Bermuda Triangle* fame), was published. Bill and I had done most of the work, finding 62 people in those pre-Internet times. By 1985 we had published about five papers, presented mostly at annual meetings of the Mutual UFO Network (MUFON). We had spoken with 92 people. We both had spoken to Dr. Jesse Marcel, and had been very favorably impressed.

Around 1988, a rather strange TV broadcast called *UFO Cover-up? Live* done in Washington, D.C., had been set up by Bill, working with Jaime Shandera, a Hollywood TV producer. Jesse was brought in for it, as was I. At the time I was living in Fredericton, New Brunswick, Canada, and Bill was living in Southern California.

I'd actually known Jaime for quite a few years. He had contacted me before I moved to New Brunswick, and had brought Bill in to help with doing a script for a short-lived movie project. They continued to work together, and kept me informed. Meanwhile, in 1978, I had been heavily involved as co–script writer, technical advisor, and on location for the production of *UFOs ARE Real*, a 93-minute documentary for Group One of Hollywood. Major Marcel was one of the people we interviewed, and that's when I finally went to Houma to meet him in person.

A number of books and documentaries have been done about Roswell since the late 1980s. One of the best was done by NBC's *Unsolved Mysteries*, for which both Jesse Jr. and I were interviewed. Some of the documentaries were by Roswell debunkers, much of whose research was often of the armchair-theorist variety. The debunkers had several basic rules, including: (A) Don't bother me with the facts, my mind is made up, (B) What the public doesn't know I won't tell them, (C) Do your research by proclamation, because investigation is too much trouble, and (D) If you can't attack the data, attack the people.

I spent a great deal of effort throughout the years dealing with the false arguments of the naysayers. The problem is that we researchers have been racing the undertaker. Inevitably, we lose, though new witnesses do turn up sometimes. As the only Roswell researcher who has been in the homes of both Jesse Sr., who died in 1986, and Jesse Jr., I have been in a better position than most to deal with the criticisms, and nobody has ever accused me of being shy about expressing my opinion when I have done my homework.

For example, I published a very strong commentary in *UFO Magazine* about the sleazy treatment of the Roswell story by the late ABC journalist Peter Jennings on February 24, 2005. Not only wasn't it noted that I was a nuclear physicist, but, though they interviewed Dr. Marcel at greater length, they didn't bother to make mention of the fact that he was a medical doctor, a flight surgeon, a helicopter pilot, and serving as colonel in the Army in Iraq when the program was finally broadcast. Any reasonable person would agree that these facts are relevant to credibility. It was almost funny that the debunkers on the show, such as SETI specialists and Harvard psychologists, had their full titles presented, despite their lack of familiarity with the evidence.

Some people have asked, "So why did all those so-called witnesses go running to Friedman and Moore? Just to get on TV?" The fact of the matter is that they didn't. We had to work hard to find the witnesses. One critic was sure that Walter Haut, who had issued the famous press release of July 8, 1947, had just made up the story and put it out on his own. Considering that the military group at Roswell was the 509th Composite Bomb Group, the most elite military group in the world, that is absurd. They had dropped the atomic bombs on Hiroshima and Nagasaki. They had hand-picked officers and high security. Some debunkers have foolishly claimed that Colonel Blanchard must have been sent to Siberia for putting out that stupid story. In actuality, he received four more promotions. At the time of his death of a massive heart attack in May 1966, he was a four-star general and vice chief of staff of the U.S. Air Force.

Another common question has been, "If security was so tight, how come Jesse Marcel was blabbing to a ham radio buddy and to UFO lecturer Stan Friedman?" That's not the case at all. Truth be told, years after my meeting with the TV station guy, I finally asked him what Jesse had actually told him about what happened. His answer was, "I asked him about the story, and he said that was something he couldn't talk about." He had read the story in the New Orleans *Times Picayune*, which mentioned that Jesse was from Houma. The most important witnesses, such as Jesse, Walter Haut, then-Colonel Thomas Jefferson DuBose, the rancher Mac Brazel, and others, all were mentioned in the contemporary press coverage. These men didn't ask for publicity, but once they got it, they could hardly deny their involvement. However, Cavitt, whom Moore and I located by

1980, wasn't mentioned in 1947, and kept avoiding telling anything useful until he gave false testimony to Colonel Richard Weaver about what he had found. Weaver's massive 1994 volume, *The Roswell Report: Fact vs. Fiction in the New Mexico Desert*, provided many official lies about the Mogul balloon explanation, as did the "crash test dummy" explanation of a second volume, *The Roswell Report: Case Closed*.

Frankly, I was pleased to be asked to contribute the foreword to Dr. Jesse Marcel Jr.'s book. The story needs to be told by someone of such high integrity as Dr. Marcel, someone who was so close to the long-ago events and people involved in them. He makes the people come alive.

The world has waited a long time for the inside scoop on Roswell. Truth is an excellent curative for false proclamations. The Roswell crashed saucer retrieval is one of the most important UFO cases ever, anywhere. We need more information from those directly involved, and this book provides a good deal of important new material.

Stanton T. Friedman
www.stantonfriedman.com
fsphys@rogers.com

INTRODUCTION

When I was 11, my life took a strange and wondrous turn late one summer night in the kitchen of my family's modest little home in Roswell, New Mexico. It was on that night that my father, Major Jesse Marcel, Sr., showed my mother and me the debris from a mysterious crash that had occurred a few weeks earlier on a ranch about 75 miles northwest of Roswell.

As we examined the debris and carefully handled it, my dad's excitement was almost palpable. Though my father was the senior intelligence officer on a base that was home to the country's most closely guarded secrets, he was, to his family, a pretty laid-back guy, who took everything in stride. But on that night, I saw another side of him. It was a mixture of excitement and confusion, suffused with a sense of wonder that one just doesn't see in many grown men. His attitude, combined with the odd nature of the material itself, made a deep impression on me. This was clearly like nothing that had been seen on Earth before. But neither my dad nor I had any notion of the profound influence that the Roswell Incident would have on the popular culture in the coming years. We certainly had no idea that the specter of Roswell would haunt our family for decades.

By most official accounts, the crash that produced the debris had occurred in mid-June of 1947. On or about June 14, William "Mac" Brazel, foreman of the Foster Ranch near Corona, New Mexico, found a large amount of what some accounts described merely as paper, rubber, and foil garbage. But my father and I have always known that it was much more than that.

When Brazel reported to the local sheriff that he might have found some wreckage from a genuine flying saucer, the sheriff contacted the Roswell Army Air Field (RAAF), where my father was stationed. My father and a Counterintelligence Corps agent, Captain Sheridan Cavitt, drove out to the ranch to examine and collect the property, and on July 8, the public information office at the RAAF announced that they had recovered the remains of a "flying disc." Not surprisingly, this caused a great stir in the media, and added fuel to the flying-saucer frenzy.

The excitement generated by the RAAF announcement was quickly deflected, however, when Brigadier General Roger Ramey at the Fort Worth Army Air Base ordered that the debris be sent to him for examination. He subsequently held a press conference, at which my father was present, and announced that the wreckage was from an errant weather balloon. My father was ordered to pose for a now-famous photograph in which he was holding some weather balloon debris. After the general's announcement, the Roswell story was dead as far as the public was concerned. But it really wasn't dead; it was merely dormant, and remained that way for more than 30 years, until a nuclear physicist and respected UFO researcher named Stanton Friedman met with my father and discussed what was *really* found that night in New Mexico. When Friedman made his findings—and my father's statements—public, Roswell once again appeared on the public radar.

For my family, the story had never really died, although my father had been ordered to keep silent about the matter. Being a good officer, he remained silent for decades, even though he knew that there were big enough holes in the "official" stories about the crash and ensuing investigation to drive a truck through. To his dying day, my father was absolutely firm in his conviction that the material we examined was as he described it, "not of this Earth," and that the truth about Roswell had yet to be revealed to the public.

In the 60 years that have passed since what has become known as the Roswell Incident, we have seen quite a parade of characters involving themselves in alternately trying to prove or dismiss the notion that the crash at Roswell was extraterrestrial in origin. Many, if not most of these people, have also been engaged in the issue of whether or not Earth has been visited by beings from another planet, or whether or not such beings even exist. Yet, for all the efforts expended by both factions, we seem to be no closer to separating fact from fiction on the subject.

This is not particularly surprising when you look at the members of each faction. On the "believers'" side, the most vocal proponents—

and, unfortunately, those who get the most media coverage—seem to belong to the "tinfoil hats" brigade. These are the people who offer such bizarre tales of abduction and the like that it is nearly impossible for any rational person to take them seriously. The most vehement members on the "naysayers'" side, however, usually use dismissal and denial—rather than actual evidence—in their attempts to refute anything that is inconsistent with their perspectives. Some, unfortunately, even resort to character attacks, as I have come to know all too well. In an attempt to bolster their arguments and refute evidence on the "pro-ET" side, some have questioned my father's credibility as well as his credentials. They have even tried to besmirch his wife, my mother, by implying that merely by being the niece of a Louisiana governor, she was somehow involved in corrupt Louisiana politics, and therefore not to be believed.

The result of the decades-long polarization and name-calling is that there has been little objective information available to those who are cautiously skeptical, as well as those open-minded skeptics who acknowledge the possibility—if not the presence of proof—that the debris found near Roswell was indeed extraterrestrial in origin. This is unfortunate not only for people who want to know the truth about Roswell, but also for all who are interested in the question of whether there is extraterrestrial life, and if so, whether the ETs have the technology to visit Earth.

To add to the confusion, it seems that all of the different factions have offered their own interpretations of events described by my father. Although some of those interpretations held reasonably close to the accounts he had given over the years, others seemed to take on a life of their own, ignoring or embellishing his actual narratives, with some of the would-be debunkers appearing to be more focused on diminishing my father's credibility than on uncovering the truth.

The true story of my father's part in the Roswell Incident, unembellished by wishful thinking and unsuppressed by political imperative, needed to be told by the one person most qualified to do so: myself. I have been asked why I have waited so long to personally publish the story of what I saw and what my father knew. I must acknowledge that this is certainly an appropriate question, and one I myself would ask of anyone in my position. The answer is quite simple. Before he passed away in 1986, my father made me promise to see the true story told. Like my father, I too had kept silent on the matter for many years, for I was, like my father, a career military man. Neither my father nor I felt at liberty to challenge the government's official version of what happened that night so many years ago, as doing so would pose a very real danger to our careers, if not our very lives. I was also consumed with the responsibilities of my medical practice (I am an ear, nose, and throat specialist), and with raising a large family. Nevertheless, since my father's death, I have attempted to tell the story via numerous interviews, only to see my words edited, twisted, and even fabricated from whole cloth. I guess I finally grew tired of seeing the truth filtered through someone else's agenda to the point that it bore little resemblance to the actual events, and decided it was time to set the record straight.

My busy life, and my own tendency to procrastinate, prevented me from sitting down and telling my father's story even after the mandate for discretion was no longer an issue. Though I had participated in countless media interviews about Roswell, the book idea was always more or less on the back burner. It was in the perilous deserts of Iraq, where I served as a flight surgeon for 13 months, from 2004 to 2005, that I was hit with a realization of urgency. Being continually in harm's way has a tendency to alter your perspective. I knew time was running out for me to keep my promise to my father; given my own age, delaying the effort any further could well put the story at risk of going untold. While still in Iraq, fueled by a sense of my own mortality, I finally began typing out my father's story. When I returned stateside, I continued my effort in earnest.

In keeping with the promise I made, I am determined to refute the allegations aimed at my father by those whose interests were apparently to perpetuate the lie, even at the cost of an honest man's reputation. To that end, included within the manuscript are previously unpublished photographs and photocopies of documents—unearthed in 2004 and 2005—which unequivocally establish my father's credentials, level of expertise, and participation as described in the events so long disputed and shrouded in mystery.

Mine is a story of actually seeing and handling artifacts from the site, of my fascination with things that neither I nor anyone else on Earth had ever beheld. I will try to communicate the depth of my father's frustration, not with those who smeared his good name, but with the complete abandonment of truth in the telling of a story so profound that it could drastically change the way we humans deal with each other. At its core, this is the story of a military officer's integrity, and a legacy of truth that must not be withheld. It is also my attempt to repay a debt to a man who taught me the value of honor, the absolute necessity of truthfulness, and the concept of respect. That such an attempt inevitably falls short of the mark is a testament to the integrity of the man himself.

To the casually curious, this book will be a source of relatively untainted information upon which they may make their own determinations about Roswell, and, possibly, about the reality of extraterrestrial life. To a government long accustomed to feeding the public information (or misinformation) however it sees fit, with little regard for the public's right to be told the truth, this book will no doubt be yet another thorn in its side. But I feel that readers deserve to know the facts, and I also believe my father deserves the respect long denied him by the government's desire to silence what he saw and knew.

Beyond my wish to see my father remembered as a man of integrity and intelligence, I feel that the public has a right to know the answer to one of the biggest questions facing us: Are we alone in the universe? The answer, firmly I believe, is no.

Another question Americans must ask is whether or not their government can be relied upon to tell them the truth, despite the potential for embarrassment that telling such truth might cause. Once again, the answer is no. Given the tenuous nature of this country's relationship with our neighbors—ally and adversary alike—it is imperative that citizens base their support upon facts, rather than convenient sound bytes or obfuscation. To do less is to shirk one's responsibility and invite disaster.

I don't pretend to have all the answers to the mystery of Roswell, nor do I pretend to be deeply knowledgeable about the technical and scientific issues surrounding the Roswell Incident or interplanetary travel. Nevertheless, I have some facts and evidence on my side, as well as a boundless curiosity about the mysteries of the universe.

My first concern is to keep my promise to my father by telling his story as it relates to the Roswell Incident. In the process, I will also tell my own story of growing up in the shadow of what is arguably the most famous event in the UFO world, and I will even share stories of how Roswell affected my own children. I will offer my views of the investigation, and a few comments about my own interactions with the media, particularly with the skeptics and naysayers, throughout the years. I have found that all too often, despite their purported rationality and scientific approach, many of the skeptics have their own agenda, and are as willing to manipulate the truth to their own interests as those whom they accuse of poor science.

What truly separates *The Roswell Legacy* from previous accounts is the absence of a specific agenda, beyond my desire to fulfill the promise made to my father: to see to it after his death that the true story is told.

So this is my father's story, and mine. It may well raise more questions than it answers, but my hope is that at the very least it will move the Roswell debate from the fringe elements to a more reasoned forum. And I hope more than anything else that in some part, my efforts will result in history remembering my father as the intelligent, honorable man that he was, rather than the obscene caricature that has so often been painted of him. He deserves no less.

June 2007

CHAPTER 1
The Path to Roswell

To know the truth about the incident in Roswell, New Mexico, in the summer of 1947, and the decades of speculation that followed, it helps to know the truth about the participants in this grand play. Much has been written about the individuals involved—some of it quite accurate, and some not so accurate. It is my hope that, after reading my account of the events as I remember them, some of those inaccuracies might be corrected.

My focus in this book is to present you with a clearer picture of the man who was—and remains—at the center of the Roswell controversy: my father, Jesse Marcel, Sr. Although I must acknowledge my own bias, I realize that my duty to my father is to present him as the man he was, as accurately as possible, lest I fall into the same trap as those who have painted an unflattering portrait of him that reflects their own biases and agendas. I feel I am the only living person truly qualified to wield the brush.

Even so, this will not be the complete story of my father's life. But it will give you some background and perspective missing in most accounts.

From Royalty to Rural Americana

In 1789, my great-grandfather and his brother, born of the royal Dauphine family, left their home in France to escape the carnage of the French Revolution. My great-grandfather moved to Louisiana, and took the name Marcell (which my father ended up shortening to its current spelling), while my great-granddad's brother apparently settled in French Canada. To my knowledge, the two brothers never saw each other again.

My father was born on May 27, 1907, in a place called Bayou Blue, in the Terrebonne Parish town of Houma, Louisiana. He was the youngest of seven siblings born to Theodule and Adelaide Marcel. Though they were in many respects an average farm family, theirs was, I am certain, an interesting household, with his mother—who as a small girl had once helped make horse collars for the Confederate Army—speaking only French, and his father raising crops. As with all farming families of that day, Jesse and his brothers and sisters worked with his parents on the farm, but unlike many other parents, his folks knew that a good education was paramount. They insisted on the children attending school, even during harvest time, when every extra hand was needed.

At an early age, my father became interested in a new device called *radio*. He read voraciously to learn all he could about this wondrous technology, and saved every penny he could until he finally had enough to buy the parts to build a radio of his own. His mother—who was of necessity a very frugal woman—would have been dead-set against wasting money on something as frivolous as this, so he had to hide the parts in a haystack. When his brother Dennis found his stash and turned him in to his mother, Dad was punished, but ended up building the radio anyway. I don't know if it worked, but I suspect it did, thus pardoning him for "wasting money."

After graduating from high school, my father knew that he wanted to continue his education, but was keenly aware of the fact that his parents were not wealthy enough to pay his way. He initially went to work for AM and JC DuPont General Store as a window dresser and stock boy, and doing other tasks as needed. While working there, he also attended classes at a graphics and design school at LSU in Baton Rouge. After working at the store for several years, he went to work for the Louisiana Highway Department, and enlisted in the Louisiana National Guard.

My father met my mother, Viaud (pronounced *vee-oh*) Aleen Abrams, in Winn Parish, Louisiana. She had a familial connection to the colorful world of Louisiana politics in the 1930s, as her uncle was Oscar Kelly ("O.K.") Allen, a member of the famous Huey P. Long political machine, and was governor of the state from 1932 until his death in office in 1936. Her mother was a full-blooded Cherokee, and the blend with my dad's French heritage made for a lively—not tumultuous—relationship. On a trip to California in June of 1935, they decided to get married before returning home in El Paso, Texas.

Not long after they were married, my parents moved to Houston, where Dad had been hired as a draftsman, drawing maps for Shell Oil Company. It was in Houston, on August 30, 1936, that I was born.

One of Dad's favorite pastimes was operating his ham radio station. In my mind, I can still hear him repeating his call sign, "William Five Charlie Yoke Item," (W5CYI) several times, and then listening across the bands to see if anyone would respond. He would spend hours at a time chewing the fat over every conceivable topic with other radio amateurs in every state in the union and all over the world. I like to believe that these signals from his transmitter are well into the interstellar medium by now. He was a member of the American Radio Relay League, an organization devoted to ham radio, and would exchange QSL cards with other amateur radio operators to document his contacts. (For those not familiar with ham radio, the three-letter Q-codes were created in 1909 by the British government as a list of abbreviations for the use of British ships and coastal stations. *QSL* means either "Do you confirm receipt of my transmission?" or "I confirm receipt of your transmission.")

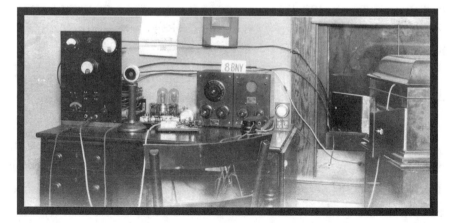

Early ham radio station (not W5CYI).

When I was only about 4 years old, half of the two-car garage at our house on Amherst Street in Houston was set up as my father's radio shack, and the rest was devoted to his small silk-screening company, where he made and sold simple signs. His home-built transmitter used mercury vapor rectifiers, the 866 vacuum tube, the venerable gas-filled tubes that would glow with a bluish color that fluctuated in brightness as he would talk. This was quite impressive to a little kid. Dad held a first-class radio operator's license, which would allow him to operate a full 1-kilowatt transmitter.

Among the hundreds of people with whom he communicated, my father made friends with some Japanese operators living in San Francisco around 1939 to 1940. He had a chance to visit them, and was astounded when he saw their equipment—huge assemblies capable of transmitting 50 kilowatts, far greater than the capacity of your typical amateur operator's rig. Their apartment, beyond being filled with a mass of radio equipment, afforded them a panoramic view of San Francisco Bay and ship movements. After the war, my father learned that his fellow "hobbyists" were actually Japanese spies. I guess that explained how they could afford such impressive equipment!

On December 7, 1941, Pearl Harbor was bombed, and shortly afterward, my father voluntarily enlisted in the Army Air Force, and soon left for Washington to take his enlistment physical.

In the summer of 1942, we moved to Harrisburg, Pennsylvania, where my father attended the Army Air Force Intelligence School. After graduating from the Intelligence School, my father was invited—inasmuch as anyone is *invited* to do anything in the military—to join the school's faculty. Many years passed before I realized what an honor it was to be so invited, an honor bestowed upon only the brightest and most talented students. That realization later became especially poignant to me, given the questions some have raised regarding my father's level of expertise and ability.

R E S T R I C T E D

SPECIAL ORDERS)   HEADQUARTERS
)   ARMY AIR FORCES AIR INTELLIGENCE SCHOOL
NO.   124)   Harrisburg, Pennsylvania 25 June 1943

- E X T R A C T -

*   *   *

14.   Following officers reld fr asgmt and dy as
students Photo Intelligence Course, AAFAIS, Harrisburg, Pa.,
effective 25 June 1943 and asgd to Shipment AF-902-A.

1ST LT JESSE A. MARCEL 0900753 AC

They WP to Kearns Field, Utah, rptng upon arrival to the CO,
Overseas Replacement Training Center, for temp dy pending
movement overseas, temperate climate.

Fifteen (15) days delay enroute authorized.

Officers will be properly immunized, have in their possession
WD MD Form 81, Pay Card Form 77, receive physical inspection as
prescribed by AR 40-100, Submit Form 43.

Relatives and friends will neither accompany officers to
Kearns Field, Utah, nor join them there later. Travel by
privately owned conveyance will not be authorized.

In lieu of subs a flat per diem of $6.00 while traveling on
official business and while absent fr perm sta within the
continental limits of the United States in accordance with
existing law and regulations is authorized.

(Auth: TWX, AC AAF, 24 June 1943)

TDN 1-5250 P 431-01-02-03-07-08 A 0425-24

*   *   *

By order of Col DAYTON:

A true copy: G W BROWNE
                                            Capt, AC
                                            Adj

JESSE A. MARCEL
1st. Lt. AC.

R E S T R I C T E D

Orders for photo intelligence school.

RESTRICTED

THIRD SPECIAL CLASS

AND SECOND SPECIAL P. I. CLASS

28 June - 8 August 1942

ARMY AIR FORCES INTELLIGENCE SCHOOL

HARRISBURG, PENNSYLVANIA

The cover sheet for intelligence school.

ARMY AIR FORCES INTELLIGENCE SCHOOL

ADMINISTRATIVE STAFF

COL. E. F. KOENIG, A. C.
Commandant

MAJ. STANTON C. AGNEW ....*Administrative Inspector*

MAJ. CHARLES O. BAIRD, JR. ....*Executive Officer*

MAJ. BILLY G. DILWORTH ....*Director of Student Administration, Combat Intelligence School*

MAJ. ERNEST T. FISH ....*Adjutant*

MAJ. JAMES W. HURT, JR. ....*Assistant Commandant*

MAJ. REGINALD C. LOMBARD, M. C. ....*Surgeon*

MAJ. JOHN H. MAXSON ....*Director of Instruction, Combat Intelligence School*

MAJ. LESTER C. CURL ....*Director of Instruction, Photo Interpretation School*

MAJ. DERRYFIELD N. SMITH ....*Director of Student Administration, Photo Interpretation School*

★ ★ ★ ★

FACULTY

Squadron Leader H. PRIESTLEY, R. A. F.

MAJ. ARNOLD WHITRIDGE	1ST. LT. FREDERICK H. DEAMANT
CAPT. CHARLES H. HALLETT	1ST. LT. JAMES L. GRIMMER
CAPT. ARTHUR A. HOUGHTON	1ST. LT. FRANK J. HANCOCK
CAPT. RALPH E. KNOWLES	1ST. LT. THEODORE S. STEVENS
CAPT. LEONARD B. LINCOLN	1ST. LT. JESSE A. MARCEL
CAPT. ALDO L. RAFFA	1ST. LT. ADOLPH M. OLSEN
CAPT. PAUL R. SMITH	1ST. LT. JACK O. BEAVER
CAPT. CUTHBERT M. MURPHY	1ST. LT. DUDLEY P. K. WOOD
CAPT. FRANKLIN P. METCALF	1ST. LT. MARSHALL L. LEWIS
CAPT. SAMUEL S. WHITT	1ST. LT. ARCHIE P. BURGESSE
CAPT. HARVEY C. BROWN	1ST. LT. EUGENE MCGUCKIN, JR.
CAPT. RICHARD C. PEASE	1ST. LT. SAMUEL L. BATCHELDER

2ND. LT. HERLEIK J. QUAMME

Intelligence school staff.

After completing his Intelligence School assignment, Dad was designated as an S-2 Intelligence Officer (his unit's principal staff officer, responsible for all military intelligence matters, including security operations, counterintelligence, training, and managing security clearance issues for personnel in his unit). His specific duties involved assessing and reporting enemy activity in the Philippines. Before he left, my parents sold the house in Houston, and my mother and I moved back to Louisiana and stayed with my grandmother at her house in Baton Rouge.

When the Japanese captured the Philippines, my father was evacuated, first to Australia, then finally back to the United States, where he was granted a short leave. One day early in 1944, I walked in the front door of our house and saw a military jacket lying on the couch. My mother was still outside unloading groceries from the car, and I ran back outside shouting, "He's here! He's here!" She dropped the bag she was holding and ran back into the house ahead of me, moving faster than I had ever seen her move before. We both plowed into the kitchen and saw him sitting there at the table, calm as you please, drinking a glass of milk and grinning from ear to ear.

The leave was brief, however, and all too soon he was assigned to the 509th Composite Bomb Group in Nevada as their S-2 intelligence officer. His pride was obvious as he told us that he was to be part of a special, hand-picked group, but he wouldn't tell us anything about what he would be doing, saying that his orders—and the work he would be doing—were classified Top Secret. Once he was settled in his new duty station, he wrote curious-sounding letters to my mother, obviously avoiding any discussion of his work in Nevada. In later years, he informed us that while he was in Nevada with the 509th, he helped to work out the details of dropping the atomic bomb on Japan.

S E C R E T

HEADQUARTERS LANGLEY FIELD

```
. . . . . . . . . . . . . . . . . . .
.       SECRET         .
.HQ LF LFVA            .
.AUTH: COA3 LFVA.      .
.DATE: 9/18/45         .
.INITIALS             .
. . . . . . . . . . . . . . . . . . .
                       rzs
```

SPECIAL ORDERS)

NUMBER   261)

Langley Field, Virginia
18 September 1945

E X T R A C T

29. Fol officers AC (9301) white qualified for overseas dy asgd orgn shown and atchd Sq H 3539th AAF Base Unit this sta (AFTRC) are reld from orgn shown and atchd Sq H 3539th AAF Base Unit this sta and WP Reception Sta indicated o/a 30 Sep 45 reporting to PDC Liaison O thereof for further disposition and asgnt.

To Camp Beale Calif (Code No 14) EDCMR 6 Oct 45

CAPT   JACK L DEVLIN   0916359   7th Ftr Wg Fort Shafter Honolulu
                                        Middle Pacific APO 958 c/o Postmaster
                                        San Francisco Calif
        Home address: 965 Portola Drive San Francisco Calif

To Fort Sam Houston Tex (Code No 10) EDCMR 4 Oct 45

MAJ   JESSE A MARCEL   0900763   43rd Bomb Gp APO 245 5th AF c/o Postmaster
                                        San Francisco Calif
        Home address: 3925 Amherst Street Houston Tex

To Fort Dix NJ (Code No 2) EDCMR 2 Oct 45

1ST LT SAMUEL G L MCDOWELL 0874670   Far Eastern AF APO 925 c/o Postmaster
                                        San Francisco Calif
        Home address: RFD #1 Marshallton Del
        Officers are auth 15 day delay enroute.
        Transportation O will furnish necessary rail and/or bus transportation.
        FDS TPA TDN A 212/60425 601-31 P 431-02 03 07 08 S 99-999
        (AUTH Secret Messageform AG 220.3 Hq AAFTTC 18 May 45)

        BY ORDER OF COLONEL MALLORY:

OFFICIAL: GILBERT E MAYEUX
                                       Capt AC
                                       Adj

JOHN T POTTER
1st Lt AC
Asst Adj
                    S E C R E T
```

Orders for overseas duty.

As the day when the bombs were to be dropped approached, the 509th was reassigned to the island of Tinian, where he participated in
```

briefing and supplying intelligence to the flight crews before the missions to Nagasaki and Hiroshima.

The Bombs That Ended the Second World War

The bomb on the left side of the following picture is "Little Boy," the uranium bomb that contained about 50 kilograms of U235 divided in separate portions. This bomb was not tested before deployment, because there was a virtual certainty that the design would work. This was the bomb carried by the *Enola Gay* that destroyed Hiroshima on August 6, 1945. The bomb on the right was "Fat Man," a plutonium bomb containing only about 10 or 12 kilograms of plutonium. The nuclear component in this bomb was only about the size of a grapefruit. Because it was not known for sure whether the implosion design would work, a test was necessary. A working device of this design was detonated in the New Mexico desert on the morning of July 16, 1945. This was the bomb carried by *Bock's Car*, which destroyed Nagasaki on August 9, 1945.

The bombs that ended WWII.

The *Enola Gay*.

After the Japanese Instrument of Surrender was signed on September 2, 1945, on the battleship *Missouri*, my father returned home to Louisiana. Upon his return stateside just after Victory Over Japan day, my dad enrolled in radar school at Langley, Virginia, where he studied advanced radar technology, becoming an expert on the state-of-the-art radar devices of that time. While there, he studied all varieties of Rawin radar targets, including the ML-307 reflector used on the Mogul device later alleged to be the source of the material found at the Roswell site.

Diploma from radar school.

Given his extensive training and familiarity with the technology of the day, the later assertion made by some that my father confused UFO debris with a radar target is ludicrous. Had he not known what a radar target (such as the Rawin reflector used on the Mogul array) looked like, he would never have been allowed to graduate from the school.

Early in 1946, we moved to Roswell, New Mexico. Dad was stationed at Roswell Army Air Field, and we lived in base housing for a while before buying a house at 1300 West Seventh Street. On one of his tours in the summer of that year, Dad participated in "Operation Crossroads," the Able and Baker tests of the atomic bombs to be detonated at Bikini Atoll. In the Able test, a 21-kiloton bomb was detonated at an altitude of 520 feet over a fleet of target ships. In the Baker test, a similar device was detonated 90 feet under water. Of the two tests, the Able test—an air burst over the test fleet—caused comparatively little damage, while the Baker (sub-surface detonation) test sank many of the ships in the test fleet.

Dad met with a gentleman by the name of Jeff Holter, who was working for the Department of Defense as a civilian scientist charged with determining wave heights and surges produced by the detonation of the atomic bombs. As it turns out, purely by coincidence, I was to become good friends with Jeff, who lived in my current home town of Helena, Montana. On one early visit to Jeff's laboratory, I noticed a picture of the Baker tests, and mentioned that my father had been there. I was quite surprised when Jeff responded, "I know. I met with him there. We even tossed back a few drinks in the Officers' Club."

My parents spent many evenings playing bridge with Major Don Yeager and his wife Helen, along with Colonel William Blanchard. They would play all night long, consuming copious amounts of their favorite beverages and chain-smoking cigarettes. They also enjoyed going to the O (Officers') Club and playing bingo on the weekends. All in all, life was normal for the times—that, of course, was destined to change dramatically in the summer of 1947.

Officer's Club at the RAAF circa 1947.

As noted earlier, I do not claim that this chapter is a comprehensive story of my father's life. That would fill an entire book by itself. My main purpose here is to give you a little background information, and to document my dad's journey into government service. Perhaps this will help answer some questions that have, on occasion, been raised about his qualifications for and participation in the events surrounding the Roswell Incident. In a later chapter I'll dig a little deeper into Roswell's lasting effects on my dad, and on our family.

What I primarily wish to convey here is that there was so much more to my father than his place as a mere footnote in history. Perhaps one day I will sit down and tell his whole story; he was a man whom I think the world needs to know. When I started looking through all of my parents' old photos and documents, I learned many things about my father that I had never known. One thing that stands out is that he was an adept wordsmith, who regularly committed his thoughts and feelings—in both poetry and prose—to his personal diary. Perhaps, if he had not been such an honorable officer, he might even have told this story himself. His dedication to the Army and his country ran deep, however, and he never wrote anything that would have run contrary to his orders to keep silent about the events that were about to transpire. Thus, he has left with me the task of seeing that the truth is told. It is a task I feel both honored and humbled to have undertaken.

The following is a short list of some of my father's awards and decorations.

➤ 15 awards for combat credit.

➤ 15 decorations and bronze service stars awarded for service.

➤ Air Medal with oak leaf cluster for operational combat flight missions from December 4, 1943, to April 23, 1944. Attached to the 65th Bomb Squadron.

➤ Soldier's Medal for meritorious achievement in military operations against the enemy in the Southwest Pacific Area from January 15, 1944 to November 1, 1944.

➤ His post-war evaluations have come under major scrutiny, especially by the skeptics trying to undermine his reputation. He was thought of very highly by his superior officers both before and after the Roswell event. His marks are generally excellent with an overall rating of high excellence. He was marked down slightly for organizational abilities, but otherwise had excellent scores. One report from one individual had him as unimaginative, but

I would think that would give him more credibility in describing the debris: If he was not imaginative, how could he have imagined debris from a weather balloon as having come from a flying saucer? David Rudiak has an excellent rundown of his evaluations on the Internet, at *www.roswellproof.com*—Major Marcel's Postwar Service Evaluations of May 6, 1948, to August 2, 1948, and General Ramey's evaluation of August 19, 1948.

➤ Vice Admiral Blandy of Operation Crossroads wrote an endorsement highly recommending Marcel for the permanent award of the Army Commendation Ribbon.

➤ In spite of what the skeptics of my dad say, the Roswell event did not affect his career, as he was promoted to lieutenant colonel in the reserves.

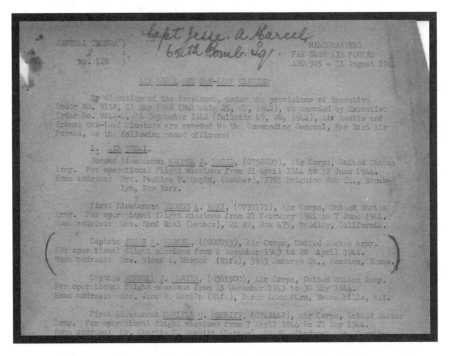

Jesse Marcel Sr.'s certificate for the Air Medal and Bronze Star.

CHAPTER 2
The Debris

The year 1947 began in a burst of optimism. Although the United States had just fought one of the bloodiest conflicts in the history of humankind, we were still relatively innocent in many ways. Life was settling back to normal after the war, and the country was moving forward with a newly robust economy. Our lives were enhanced by modern conveniences that had only been dreamed of a few years earlier. We were in total control of our destiny, and the sky was the limit where our standard of living was concerned. Those were good times in my life, simple times when little boys could play and dream and aspire to greatness, seemingly limited only by their imaginations. Little did I know, however, that things were about to change beyond anything I could possibly have imagined, and that the world I knew would never again be as simple.

I turned 11 that year, and similar to a lot of kids my age, I was interested in aviation. The dashing aces who had torn up the skies during the two World Wars were my heroes, and stick-built models of the airplanes they had flown hung from the ceiling of my bedroom at various attitudes. My favorite models were the WWI biplanes such as the British SPAD, and the German Fokker triplane flown by Baron Manfred von Richthofen, the famous "Red Baron." (When Chuck Yeager broke the sound barrier with the Bell X-1 on October 14 of that year, a model of his Bell X-1 joined the other models hanging from my ceiling.) And even though my dad wasn't one of the legendary aces, he did dream of becoming a pilot, and took his place pretty near the top of the list of my heroes. Although he never actually got his license, he did have a good amount of "bootleg" time in the right seat. I remember him telling us of a time when he was landing a B-25 Mitchell like those used on the Doolittle Tokyo raid, when he came in too low with a heavy load and almost collapsed the landing gear. No significant damage was done to the airplane or its cargo, but his pride took a bit of a beating. I remember him saying the aircraft was carrying a heavy safe and he almost landed underneath the runway.

Most days, I could be found riding around my neighborhood on my bicycle. But in those magical times, it wasn't a bicycle at all, but a

Fokker, screaming across the skies over France, and I was the dashing Baron, striking fear in the hearts of my enemies and wonder in the eyes of my fellow aces. In my mind, I could hear the thunder of the engine as I swooped down on my prey, proud raptor in wood and fabric, the heat of the exhaust turning the oil spray to mist on the goggles I had purchased at the five-and-ten-cent store. I was, in those innocent times, the true lord of the skies.

In the cool of the evening, when darkness drove all aces to ground, we would chase the fireflies as they flitted across the blackness, or search for the strange insects and lizards that came out once the din of our aerial battles was silenced. So many years have passed since those days and nights. I am what most people would consider an old man now, but when I close my eyes, I am still a little boy, drinking deep from the well of wonder that seems to run dry as we get older. I may tend to forget little things that happened to me yesterday or the day before, but I can still remember the sounds, the smells, and the sky that burned brighter and clearer in daylight than any I've seen since, and that by night held a darkness that must only exist in this inexplicable place, and on planets beyond the reach of grownups and their machines.

But something was happening in our skies that summer that shattered the simplicity of the times and defied explanation. How much was real and how much was the product of the public's overly active imagination is something on which no one can agree, even today. In June, there had been dozens of reports of strange objects flitting through the air, which most observers described as *flying saucers* or *flying discs*. For instance, Kenneth Arnold was a civilian pilot who was flying around Mt. Rainier that month, looking for a downed aircraft, when a reflection of sunlight caught his attention. As he looked in the direction of Mt. Baker, he saw nine boomerang- or crescent-shaped

Main Street, Roswell, circa 1947.

objects flying in formation near the mountaintop, apparently traveling at a tremendous speed. He likened them to saucers skipping over
the surface of water, but when he tried to close in on them they were
traveling much too fast. That was one week before something crashed
to the ground outside of Roswell, New Mexico. Not long after that
there was a report of an unknown object being picked up on radar-
scopes at Alamogordo and White Sands. The next day there were
various eyewitness reports of a glowing object traveling in the area of
Roswell heading toward the northwest.

About that time I recall seeing an intense blue-white light traveling to the northwest over Roswell one evening as I looked up while
going into the house. I did not put much meaning into that sighting,
so accustomed was I to the magic of being a boy growing up in the
desert, until I learned of other people reporting basically the same
thing. I began to wonder if there might be lords of other skies

unknown to us, who had come to pay a visit to the men who reigned supreme beneath this sun.

The event that was to change my father's life—and mine—happened one stormy summer evening at the Foster Ranch near Corona, New Mexico, about 75 miles north of Roswell. The foreman of that ranch, William "Mac" Brazel, heard a sound like some sort of explosion. The sound was apparently heard on another ranch some 10 to 12 miles away. Mr. Brazel reported that the noise was strong enough to rattle the windows in the ranch house for a short time. The thunderstorms in the area that night were pretty severe, and goodness knows the summertime storms around Roswell were frequently intense, with high wind and copious amounts of rain. The storms usually came on very quickly, and the skies would clear just as suddenly. I recall one afternoon I went to a movie at the Plains Theater with a friend when a cloudburst just west of Roswell started up. By the time we got out of the movie, people were using boats to go down Main Street.

There is no doubt in my mind that Mr. Brazel was well aware of the sounds generated by thunderstorms, particularly because the ranch house had been hit by lightning in the past. But this sound was different from anything produced by a thunderstorm or a lightning strike. This sounded more like what I imagined to be a large bomb exploding.

Mac Brazel said that the following morning, he saddled his horse and rode out to look for what could have possibly caused the loud explosion, and to check the area for any damage. To his surprise, he came across an area that was littered with, among other things, a huge amount of foil-like debris. Something had apparently impacted the ground at a high rate of speed and fanned its components into a wedge-shaped field of wreckage. A large herd of sheep was stranded on one side of the debris field; the sheep refused to cross it, even though their water supply was on the other side. Mr. Brazel ended up having to lead them around the area so they could get to the water. Some reports say he gathered up some of the debris and brought it to a neighboring ranch, where a woman named Loretta Proctor lived. She reportedly suggested to him that there might be some kind of a reward for turning the material in, so a short time later—I am not sure exactly when, as there are varying stories—he went into the nearby town of Corona.

It was there that he heard stories of strange flying machines invading the skies. Although Mr. Brazel had previously seen debris from weather balloon crashes on the Foster Ranch property, this material looked different. Very different. And after listening to the tales of the flying saucers, he became convinced that maybe the stuff he had discovered was part of one of these strange machines.

Brazel thought the local sheriff's office would be the appropriate place to reveal what he'd discovered. He figured he'd let Sheriff Wilcox examine it and decide what to do. But the sheriff could not make any definitive judgment on what it was, so he contacted the command at the Roswell Army Air Field. Colonel William Blanchard, the base commander, had my dad go over to the sheriff's office to see what Brazel had brought in. My father was the base intelligence officer, and, as such, part of his job was to be on an investigative team for aircraft accidents, or any problem that arose with security. The base was part of the SAC (Strategic Air Command), and was responsible for the nuclear weapons housed there.

My father looked the debris over and determined that it was indeed bizarre—certainly out of the ordinary—and merited further examination. When Colonel Blanchard got my dad's report on the unusual nature of the material, he had Dad and Captain Sheridan "Cav" Cavitt, a counterintelligence agent (in the CIC), accompany Mr. Brazel back to the ranch so they could see for themselves what was there. They went in separate vehicles, my dad going in the family car, a 1942 blue Buick Special convertible, and Cavitt going in a military carryall. The ranch was about 75 miles away, on roads that had seldom seen cars. They arrived early in the evening, and decided to spend the night at the ranch and inspect the debris field the next day. The following morning, the three of them went to the see what was out there.

Once at the debris field, instead of being able to get answers for Colonel Blanchard, they only unearthed more questions. The debris field was very large, and, as I mentioned earlier, wedge-shaped, or perhaps I should say fan-shaped. There was a scar at the apex of the fan, which spread out for several hundred yards to a considerable width at the end of the field.

My dad was not entirely satisfied with the debris that had already been collected, so he directed Captain Cavitt to go on to the base while he went back out and collected more of the material. (In retrospect, I wonder if he had Capt. Cavitt go on ahead so he could then bring the debris to our house without calling attention to his side trip.) He placed the debris in a box in the back seat of our 1942 Buick, and more in the trunk. Even with all of the material he gathered, he said that this was only a small portion of what was found.

My father knew that what he had found was something absolutely incredible, and even though speaking of it might not have been condoned by his base commander, he knew that it was important to share what he had seen with my mother and me. And that's how the debris ended up in the kitchen of our little house at 1300 West Seventh Street.

I remember that kitchen so well, with its white cupboards and white-and-gold linoleum. If you came into the kitchen through the back door, as we often did, the sink was to the left, the stove and refrigerator to the right. A swinging door led into the dining room. My memory of that night is as clear as my memory of the details of our house. As it was summertime, the back door was open to let in fresh air. The temperature outside was in the upper 60s, and the air was slightly humid because of yet another recent thunderstorm.

As the base intelligence officer, my father kept rather odd hours, and it was not unusual for him to be gone for days. He had left for work the previous morning and hadn't been home for dinner the previous night or this one. I don't remember what time it was when my father awakened me, but I had been sleeping soundly for some time, weary after a day of bicycling with my friends. More than likely it was a little after midnight. My dad came into my room to tell me to come out and see what he'd found. He said that he had been out to a ranch and had picked up debris from something that had crashed there. As I recall, he was still in uniform because he was going back to the base that night. (In fact, I seldom if ever saw him in civilian clothes unless we were on vacation.) Of course, it wasn't normal for my father to wake me up late at night just to show me something, so I immediately put my robe on and followed him into the kitchen area.

I only later found out that the details about how he and Captain Sheridan Cavitt had been sent out to the Foster Ranch to examine the wreckage of an unknown craft of some sort. All I knew this night was that he was pretty excited about something, that he thought it was an extraordinary event, and he wanted my mother and me to be part of it. My mother was already up as I walked down the dimly lit hallway that led to the living room and then to the kitchen. Upon reaching the kitchen, the first thing I noticed was a cardboard box that had been mostly emptied, with the contents positioned carefully on the floor. The box was a standard 2-by-2 in size, so it could hold only a moderate amount of debris, but there was still enough material to cover a significant portion of our kitchen floor.

My dad spoke very excitedly to us about the material, telling us that these were parts from a "flying saucer," or words to that effect. At that time, I was not entirely sure what was meant by a "flying saucer," but I knew from his demeanor that this was something very special.

I looked wide-eyed at the debris that was spread out on the floor, along with what little had been left in the box, and quickly determined that there were three different kinds of material present: foil, broken pieces of plastic, and what appeared to be metal beams, or I-beams.

The brownish-black plastic looked similar to pieces of Bakelite (a plastic used in countertops in the 1940s), or perhaps a broken phonograph record. Actually, the material was lighter than Bakelite, and whereas Bakelite is a fibrous material, this had more of a homogeneous structure to it. The pieces I saw were about 1/16 of an inch thick, with fractured edges, yet I don't recall seeing any fractures in the material itself. The surface was smooth, with no wrinkles, grooves, or indentations. The largest piece was about 6 or 8 inches square, with most pieces being 3 or 4 inches. There was not nearly as much of this as there was of the foil. The I-beams, at first glance, appeared to be made from the same material as the foil, but they were more substantial.

Even though the material was pretty interesting, I have to admit that I still didn't really understand what all the excitement was about. It surely did not seem to be anything worth getting up in the middle of the night to see. But my dad was really excited about it, and he wasn't the type to get that excited about just anything. So I took a closer look at the debris.

Dad asked my mom and me to look for any electronic components, such as vacuum tubes, resistors, condensers, or wire. After we searched through all the materials, we all agreed there was nothing that appeared to be part of any electronic equipment, but I feel he already knew that and wanted us to confirm it.

My attention then focused on the foil, mainly because there was more of it than anything else. The foil was similar to the aluminum kitchen wrap of today, but appeared to be stronger, and it felt lighter than a feather in my hand. Although it looked like kitchen foil at first glance, it was more substantial, and seemed to be less malleable. When I picked it up, I noticed it did not have a paper backing for rigidity, as would the foil of a radar target (which others later said it was). The largest piece I saw was perhaps 6 or 8 inches across, and the edges were irregular, with sharp tears covering the entire perimeter of the pieces. Even though I was curious, I did not try to bend or tear it. After all, this was some kind of precious material, and, as my father had told us, we were probably some of the first humans to see it.

Later, when my father was examining the material back at the base, he mentioned that when he bent or folded a piece of the foil, it would return to its original shape when released. Apparently there were larger pieces of the foil that I did not see, and these larger pieces were nearly indestructible. My dad described how one of the men from his office took a sledge hammer and hit one of the large pieces, but could not make a dent in it or deform it in any way. The sledge hammer simply bounced off the piece. If this man is still alive, I wonder where he is today; as far as I know, he was never interviewed, and never came forward during the many investigations of the Roswell Incident.

The foil had a more or less dull appearance, similar to a burnished aluminum surface, not shiny or highly reflective, although one side may have been more polished than the other. The surface of the foil itself was somewhat smooth. The pieces didn't have any distinct design or shape; they were amorphous. I remember looking at some of the foil material for quite a while. In particular, I remember how light it was—if you dropped it, it would float like a feather.

My dad said, "Let's take some of the pieces and try to fit them together like a jigsaw puzzle." So the three of us got down on our hands and knees and tried to fit the pieces together, but could find no two pieces that would interlock. We couldn't make any kind of outline that would make sense, and as there were simply too many pieces of the puzzle to fit any of them together, we finally gave up.

As I mentioned before, my father had told us to look for anything that could be associated with electronics, such as vacuum tubes, condensers, resistors, or wire. What he really wanted us to do was to look for pieces of a radio. I plowed through the debris, but could not find anything related to a radio—not even anything that resembled staples, rivets, fasteners, and so on.

In fact, there were no electronic components whatsoever in the debris I saw, or in any of the other material recovered from the site. My dad was pretty well apprised of what was in the debris, and there was no mention of electronic components by anyone, or in any of the released photos of the debris.

Fifty years later, the official Air Force publication, *The Roswell Report: Case Closed*, explained that the debris was not from a weather balloon, as first reported, but from what was called a *Mogul balloon*. The Mogul balloon was highly classified, not for its off-the-shelf components, but for its purpose: It was designed to pick up sonic vibrations in the atmosphere from any distant nuclear explosion, especially those that might occur in the Soviet Union. Skeptics point out that because Mogul balloons were indeed highly classified, naturally there would have been a cover-up by the government.

Had it been a weather balloon or a Mogul balloon, however, there would have been electronic components. Weather balloon debris would have contained a radio transmitter, as well as special sensors to detect and record weather data. A Mogul balloon would have had a radio transmitter and microphones to detect pressure waves in the atmosphere from a possible Soviet nuclear test. But these things were nowhere to be found in any of the debris. There were certainly no such components in the material I saw, and my dad said there had been none in any of the rest of the material collected from the field.

In the years since then, I have been asked many questions about this debris, such as whether there were any strings, twine, or wire in the material I saw. There were not. Yet these types of material would absolutely have been present in a Mogul balloon or even a weather balloon, as they were used to help hold the balloon together.

Years later, I had a conversation with Air Force officials, and I asked them point-blank if the brownish-black plastic I described could have been the housing for a radiosonde, a radio transmitter hoisted aloft by an array of balloons in order to take a variety of measurements. A modern radiosonde will measure barometric pressure, altitude, geographic coordinates, temperature, relative humidity, wind speed, and direction. They replied that those were either made of aluminum or cardboard—never plastic. In the end, they admitted they did not know what I saw.

I also saw what looked like a metallic beam sticking out of the box. There were several of these beams in the box, with the longest being about 18 inches and the shortest about 12 inches. I picked the larger beam out of the box and took a long look at it, holding it over my head to get a better perspective of it in the ceiling light. The material looked similar to a kite stick, except it was made of metal. It somewhat resembled an I-beam used in building construction. It was only 3/8 of an inch wide, and was a dull gray metallic color. The beam's central portion was about 1/16 of an inch, with the shoulders of the I-beam forming a ridge along its length.

I figured this was something that added structural rigidity to whatever it came from. The material itself seemed to be identical to the foil, just in a structural form. It was also incredibly light for its size. I didn't try to bend the metal; rather, I handled it carefully. Knowing how a young boy's mind sometimes worked, my father reminded me to be careful with the material. "After all," he said, "this is government property now, and I don't want to have to explain how my 11-year-old son destroyed it." His scolding was good-natured, as was his way, but I got the message nonetheless.

I don't remember if the ends of the I-beam were clean-cut or fractured like a break. I tend to think now that they were cleanly cut, but cannot be certain of my memory here.

I did notice something unusual about the inside surface of the I-beam. I caught a glint of color on the inner surface—kind of a purplish violet hue with a metallic tinge. This surface was somewhat shiny and reflective when light was shown directly on it. As I looked at the piece, with the light reflecting on the inner surface, I could see what looked like writing. At first I thought of Egyptian hieroglyphics, but there were no animal outlines or figures. They weren't mathematical figures either; they were more like geometric symbols—squares, circles, triangles, pyramids, and the like. Approximately 1/4 of an inch tall, they were imprinted on the inner surface of the beam, and only on one side. They were not engraved into the I-beam, but seemed more like part of its surface.

There were about 30 symbols, one right after another. These figures were solid; they were not line drawings. I don't recall what all of the symbols looked like or whether or not they repeated themselves. I do distinctly remember a few of them, however. One reminded me of a seal balancing a ball on its nose. The symbol was like a truncated pyramid with a solid ball over the apex, sort of like the pyramid with an eye over it on a dollar bill. I recall this symbol as being located more toward one end of the beam. The symbol located just to the right of this was an oblate spheroid. The spheroid sometimes would appear with two smaller spheroids below the larger spheroid, and sometimes above. As I recall, the next symbol had the same configuration, but it was reversed 90 degrees. To the right of these symbols was a simple oval, with the largest area of the oval being through the center section. Most of the individual symbols were about the same height and width. The symbols themselves were very close together—almost touching, but not quite.

I called my findings to the attention of my folks, showing my mother first because my dad was standing off to one side. They passed the I-beam back and forth between the two of them. At this point, I was getting a little excited, wondering what the symbols might represent. They seemed strange indeed. My dad was quite interested in the beam, and felt that the symbols might represent an alphabet of some sort. For me this was the centerpiece of the whole experience. Later I tried to reproduce the symbols I had seen, but could only draw a rough representation of what they looked like. The only one I clearly remember for sure is the truncated pyramid with a solid ball over the top of it, and I suppose that was because I could tie it in to a familiar object—a seal balancing a ball on its nose.

Picture of an I-beam replica created by Miller Johnson, who can be contacted at akjac@comcast.net.

Years later, shortly before my dad died, we discussed the shapes and colors of the symbols. I asked, without hinting to him, "What color were they?" He responded, "Oh, they were a purplish color with what looked like some kind of weird language in the form of strange shapes." His memories of the symbols were very much in sync with mine.

There was one other type of debris, though, that I didn't see in the material my dad brought home, but he said it was in some of the other debris. Many years later, he told my wife, Linda, that there were fine strands resembling fishing line in some of the material. These could very possibly have been a type of fiber optics.

I recall that Bill Brazel, Mac Brazel's son, also described seeing what he called fishing line in some of the debris. He went so far as to say that when a light was shown on one end, it was transmitted to the other end similar to a fiber-optic cable. However, as I've said, I never encountered anything like that in the debris that my father brought home.

Some UFO enthusiasts see significance in the fact that there were pretty dramatic advancements in fiber technology in the years immediately after the crash. Indeed, in the late 1940s and early 1950s, fiber-optic technology took a great leap forward. But I tend to think that's just a coincidence. There's really nothing mysterious about the development of fiber optics; it can be traced right back to the people who developed it. We humans are pretty smart, after all, and don't need help from our extraterrestrial friends to make scientific advancements.

Another question I have been asked throughout the years is whether or not there was any kind of smell associated with any of the wreckage. I don't remember any kind of smell whatsoever. Had it been Bakelite, it would have had a very distinctive smell because of the bonding agent that holds it together. And apparently the balloons that were used in Project Mogul emitted a very strong odor of neo-prene as well. But there was no odor whatsoever from the materials my father brought home.

After we had looked at the debris for about 15 or 20 minutes, we placed the material back in the cardboard box it came in, and I ac-companied my dad outside as he put the box into the back seat of our car. Standing next to the car, I noticed that the trunk was open. It was dark, and I couldn't make out a whole lot of details, but I could see that there were several more boxes of debris in the trunk.

We all went back into the house, and my mother swept the floor, because some small pieces of the materials were still on it. Therefore, a few tiny fragments were just swept out our back door. We had re-cently laid a concrete slab at the door for a washing machine; had this incident happened before we laid the slab, some of the material might have been preserved under the concrete, and perhaps could have later been retrieved by investigators. But by the time Roswell captured the attention of the world again, those minute fragments were long gone.

My mother and I retired to our respective bedrooms, and my dad took off for the base at that time, or early that morning, with his precious cargo. He had a very long day ahead of him. As I've noted, Dad had shown my mother and me only a small portion of the debris that was collected on the Foster Ranch, and there was much more investigation to be done.

After the debris was taken to the base, apparently Colonel Blanchard had a look at it and ordered the material to be flown to Fort Worth so General Ramey, the 8th Air Force commander, could inspect it. It was flown in a B-29 under armed guard. The plane had to fly at low alti-tudes because the guards were in the unpressurized cargo compart-ment with the debris. My dad was also on that flight, and it was he who displayed the debris to Ramey in his office. Ramey had him point out on a map the exact location where the debris was collected, then ordered it to be flown to Wright-Patterson Army Air Field in Dayton, Ohio.

When my dad returned to Roswell, he cautioned my mother and me never to tell others what we had seen that night. In talking with him later, he confirmed that this material was from an unearthly craft, and I was certainly convinced of this myself. My father had gone to radar and intelligence school, so he was pretty well versed in the types of radar targets of the day. This debris was not from anything he had ever seen. But there was more to it than that. It seems that he had seen other things that convinced him that this was not of human manufacture. I didn't know what made him so strong in his beliefs, but because I had seen some pretty unusual features in the debris myself, and I trusted my father's expertise, it didn't take much to convince me that he was right.

Later, when we talked about the crash site, he described a large area heavily scattered with metallic debris from a single impact point that scarred the earth. The material spread out from this point into a triangular-shaped area 200 to 300 feet wide at the end of the field, and 3/4 of a mile long. As far as the volume of the debris, just to give you an idea, they had to use a C-54 Skymaster—a large cargo aircraft—to transport it all. I later found out that the pilot of the aircraft was a Captain Henderson, who apparently saw far more than just the debris from the impact site. Based on some interviews with his family, he may in fact have seen the remains of a crew.

Although I had been told not to talk with my friends about this matter, that did not keep me from going over in my mind the significance of what I had seen. I know that my dad had been very excited about the debris, and I clearly recall him using the words *flying saucer* in reference to the materials. Even though he was the epitome of discretion after that, I never forgot that night in our kitchen.

And how could I not be excited? I have never really been a fan of science fiction, but this was not fiction. For me this was science reality, and it was a more exciting reality than any of the science I had learned in school. It was an event that definitely changed me. From that evening on, my life took on a different meaning. I could never look at the night sky the same way again, because, for all I knew, someone else might be looking back.

CHAPTER 3
Government Cover-Up?
You Decide

I n the 200-plus years of the history of our government and military, there is no other incident for which—even after 60 years have passed—the government has continued to devote time and money to keep the truth of the event from the public. Had the materials found near Roswell in 1947 actually been a weather balloon, as the government initially claimed, subsequent attempts to contest the official story would have merely been ignored as the ramblings of a few unbalanced conspiracy theorists. And even if the materials had been part of a project that was classified at the time—such as the then-Top-Secret Mogul balloon—the constant evolution of technology (not to mention the end of the Cold War) would have rendered such a classification moot. Even the technology involved in the most closely held secret of the 20th century, the development in Los Alamos of the atomic bomb, is now readily available in reference books found in every public library, as well as on hundreds of Websites. To claim an ongoing need to conceal the facts surrounding a 60-year-old defensive system is, at best, quaint. To continue to expend efforts to maintain secrecy around it is not only ludicrous, but it also calls into question the motivation of those so obsessed with the efforts.

I am well aware that the "official" reports, including the 1997 Air Force opus, *The Roswell Report: Case Closed*, claim that the cat is out of the bag, so to speak, and there is no cover-up anymore. Needless to say, I disagree, and in this chapter I'll give a more detailed explanation of why that is.

Initially, the government claimed that it had recovered a flying disk on a ranch outside of Roswell, but within 24 hours, the story began to change. The new story was that a weather balloon had fallen to earth, rather than a flying disc, and that the public's excitement about the incident was therefore unjustified. According to the revised statements, it was just a case of mistaken identification resulting from the fact that the officers on the recovery team did not know what the components of a weather balloon looked like. I find it amusing that the same government who had paid for my father to attend advanced radar school, where he was required to gain intimate familiarity with radar targets of all types, claimed that he could not recognize a radar target from a weather or Mogul balloon. Were it not for the fact that my father's reputation suffered as a result of these absurdly false statements, perhaps I could enjoy the irony.

When my father examined the debris from the crash site, he knew that it had not come from a weather balloon or radar target, and he reported as much to his commanding officer, Colonel Blanchard, who agreed with his assessment. After Colonel Blanchard had performed his own examination and submitted his report, he had the base information officer issue a public statement, the infamous "flying disc" news report. In the decades that have passed since the event, some have even stated that my father immediately rushed to the press with the story. Obviously, those who would make such allegations knew neither my father nor the dictates of military protocol. In truth, any intelligence officer who made public any potentially controversial information would have faced immediate disciplinary action, especially in the tense environment so pervasive in those early days of the cold war. My father was well aware of this, and the fact that he faced not disciplinary action, but continuously high praise in his subsequent performance evaluations, should put such allegations to rest, once and for all.

In short order, Colonel Blanchard was contacted by General Ramey, the Commander of the 8th Air Force, and ordered to issue a "corrected" statement, in which the material was to be described as debris from a common weather balloon. Blanchard was also ordered to immediately fly the debris to the general's office at Fort Worth Army Air Field so Ramey could examine it himself. General Ramey further specified that my father was to accompany the material on the flight. Once my father had arrived with the debris, General Ramey arranged for a civilian journalist to come to the base and photograph the materials. Following are two of the famous photos taken by photographer James Bond Johnson for the *Fort Worth Star-Telegram*.

My dad displaying debris from a radar target.

General Ramey inspecting radar target debris.

The pictures taken in General Ramey's office showed remnants of a genuine Rawin radar target, which is a special type of target tied beneath a free balloon and designed to be an efficient reflector of radio energy. Although you may not be able to see it clearly in the photo, the balloon envelope—the packaging that holds a balloon prior to its being deployed—was also in the background. This is the picture that was released to the public to reinforce the government's contention that there was no reason for excitement. My father was ordered to appear in the photograph holding the weather balloon material for one reason: to support the Army's contention that the officers who had made the initial determination had erred because they did not really know what they were looking at. In the first photograph, my father is shown holding a portion of a radar target, and the look on his face says it all: "They've got to be kidding!"

The report the government issued had been carefully constructed. My father was asked to hold what was obviously a remnant of a radar target, with the implication that this was the debris retrieved from the Foster Ranch that my father had showed us in our kitchen. He was further ordered to keep silent, and not to make any comments in the presence of the civilian photographer. I think it was at this time that my dad realized that the cover-up had begun, and that he was going to be stuck in the middle of it, whether he liked it or not.

Besides the look on my father's face, others things in the photograph simply don't add up. The government claimed that the materials shown in the photograph were the retrieved remnants of the crashed balloon, but I'd like to know where that balloon envelope came from. As I mentioned earlier, the envelope is the packaging the balloon is housed in pre-deployment, so a balloon envelope would never be present at a crash site, and the envelope was certainly not part of the debris flown in from Roswell. Obviously, it had to be placed in the photo with the rest of the switched debris to reinforce the idea that the material found at the site was a weather balloon with its accompanying radar target. They even had a weather balloon expert come in and testify—correctly—that the material in the photograph was the remnant of a weather balloon. In short, they pulled out all the stops to confirm their story.

Another interesting point is that others in the office—including the civilian photographer—later reported that the debris photographed in the office had a strong odor of something that had been burned. As I noted in the last chapter, however, there was no odor whatsoever associated with the debris we inspected in our kitchen that night.

Dad later told us that the civilian photographer saw only a small part of the actual debris, and that he was only allowed to observe the *real* debris—which remained wrapped up—from a distance, as opposed to being allowed to get close enough for a detailed photograph, as he had been allowed to do with the radar target material. Does this mean that there was a mix of genuine debris with debris from a weather balloon? This is indeed what happened, as the foil shown in the photograph was paper-backed, and looked like tin foil and balsa wood sticks, whereas the foil on our kitchen floor did *not* have a paper backing. In a later interview, the photographer remarked that General Ramey—who would certainly have been able to identify weather balloon materials—had no idea what the materials were. Johnson, the photographer, said, "While shooting the general, I asked him what all this material was. He shrugged and answered something like, 'Damned if I know.'"

One of the other photographs was quite interesting as well. In it, General Ramey was shown holding what appears to be a telegram, and, as it happened, the printing on the telegram was partially facing the camera. David Rudiak analyzed the telegram, and through computer enhancements (see the following pictures), there are several words that can be made out. Those words included the phrases "victims of the," and "emergency powers needed." One would think that if the telegram had been describing just the downing of a weather balloon, words such as "victims of the" would not be applicable, as there are generally no *victims* in the wreck of a weather balloon. The other words were suspicious as well, mentioning the necessity of emergency powers being needed at Site Two, which was southwest of Magdalena, New Mexico. The intensity of the Army's dismissal, combined with the phrases gleaned from the telegram, certainly made it sound as if something other than a simple weather balloon—or even a secret observation device—had been discovered at Site Two.

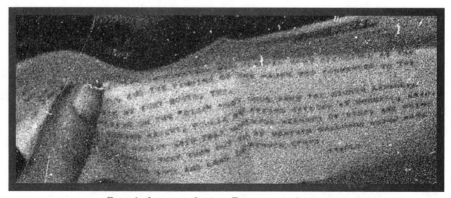

Breakdown of the Ramey telegram.

The government admitted much later that there had been a cover-up after all. In their later statements, they claimed that what was recovered from Roswell was not from a weather balloon, but in reality was debris from a Top Secret project, the so-called Mogul balloon, which, as I explained in the last chapter, was designed to detect atmospheric disturbances caused by Soviet nuclear tests. This subsequent

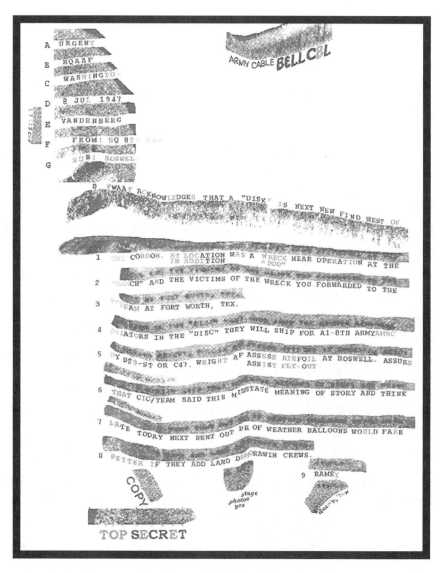

Enlargement of the Ramey telegram.

explanation highlights yet another rather obvious flaw in the official story: Under no circumstances would the government publish pictures of its Top Secret projects on the cover page of press releases, at least not while the information was still classified. Hence, openly publishing such pictures at that time smelled of cover-up as well. In the next chapter, I'm going to go into more detail about Mogul balloons. For now, though, I want to stress that, even though the Mogul balloon *project* was classified, the materials used in it were not. In fact, they were off-the-shelf items; only their intended use was Top Secret. My father surely would have recognized these common components, yet in its attempt to bolster its story, the government implied rather clearly that my father did not recognize any of these common components.

And that is patently absurd. As I stated before, my father had just gone through radar school, where he studied radar targets similar to the one he was ordered to hold for the photo session. In essence, the government implied that my father couldn't even tell the difference between a box kite and a P-51 Mustang. Such claims just made no sense.

Of the 11 flights of the Mogul project in 1947—and again, I'll go into more detail in the next chapter—the government's story focused upon Flight #4, which was launched on June 3. Based upon prevailing winds and atmospheric conditions that day, the projected flight path would not have taken the balloon anywhere near the crash site.

Immediately after the debris was moved to Fort Worth, both my father and Colonel Blanchard were "offered" the opportunity to take a three-week leave of absence. This could have been for reasons unrelated to the discovery and ensuing cover-up, but my father felt that it certainly was suspect, especially because he wasn't allowed to come home for those three weeks. Instead, he inadvertently became part of the cover-up, spending this period being debriefed on what he saw, as well as how to handle the public and other government agencies' inquiries. According to records later made available, Colonel Blanchard had scheduled his own leave prior to the crash, but he apparently used the time to go back to the crash sites to have a look.

By July 10, 1947, all of the debris had been vacuumed (my father's words) from the crash site and moved to Wright-Patterson Air Force Base in Dayton, Ohio. The aircraft used to transport the debris was a C-54. It took an aircraft of large size to transport the considerable amount of debris, as well as the number of armed guards needed to ensure that the debris was not seen by anyone not directly involved in the government's explanation of the event.

If the government were only transporting the wreckage of a Mogul balloon, it would not have needed an aircraft the size of a C-54, let alone guards to protect the over-the-counter materials that made up the balloons and instruments.

Inasmuch as the debris from Mogul balloons recovered by research teams were typically disposed of without any special security measures taken, why would the government have felt the need to transport what they found on the Foster Ranch under guard on a special flight? Obviously, the material being transported was *not* the remnants of a Mogul balloon.

Later, the pilot of the aircraft, Captain Pappy Henderson, recalled the flight and mentioned the large crate used to haul the materials, and, according to Henderson, the alien bodies. Neither my father nor I ever saw any alien bodies, but as you probably know, several other people did make that claim.

Interestingly enough, all records from Roswell pertaining to the recovery of the debris are no longer available, reportedly having been inadvertently destroyed, lost, or misplaced. I can't help wondering who was responsible for those records, and why only these particular items are missing. Perhaps they were abducted by aliens.

The Government Tries to Close the Case

As of today, the government is still holding to its story, although the particulars of that story have changed many times in the years since the crash occurred. In 1994, the government issued the first of several special reports on Roswell. The final version was issued in 1997; it was a 213-page document called *The Roswell Report: Case Closed*, which purported to finally tell the truth, the whole truth, and nothing but the truth about the Roswell event. The report was based on an exhaustive search for records about Roswell, the purpose being to determine if the Air Force or any other U.S. government agency had information on the crash and recovery of an extraterrestrial vehicle and its alien occupants.

Besides revealing what the crash was, the document discusses what the crash *wasn't*. Here's what it says the Roswell Incident was not.

An Airplane Crash

As anyone who watches television, listens to the radio, or reads a newspaper knows, airplane crashes are big news, and even the most minor of such incidents is both officially documented and publicly described. The only crashes that have any chance of escaping extensive public scrutiny are those involving classified military missions or test flights. Between the dates of June 24, 1947, and July 28, 1947, there were a total of five crashes officially documented in New Mexico, none of which occurred on the dates or in the vicinity of the Roswell debris site.

Incidentally, the government report also examined how the different agencies documented crashes of weather balloons and other non-typical aerial vehicles. Inasmuch as a "crash" or uncontrolled landing is the *normal* means of terminating a weather balloon flight, the only time a report of such an event is documented is when the falling debris causes injury or property damage. Even these records are only maintained for five years.

A Missile Crash

There have been some who have theorized that the Roswell Incident was actually the crash of a missile, such as a previously captured German V-2. Given the fact that any such tests—which would have been launched at nearby White Sands missile range— were classified as Secret at the time, the government would have handled such crashes under tight security, especially if the flight had crashed on land not under government control. Air Force records, however, do not suggest that such a crash could have been involved in the Roswell case. At any rate, there would be no pressing need to maintain a classified status involving tests on World War II–era weaponry, as virtually all technical information pertaining to these weapons is publicly available anyway.

A Nuclear Accident

Because in 1947, the 509th Bomb Group was the only military unit in the world that possessed nuclear weapons, it would be understandable for one to question whether the Roswell Incident might have been somehow associated with nuclear weapon–related tests. Extensive reviews of available records—even those still classified Top Secret—gave no indication that this was the case. Also, any records pertaining to nuclear incidents eventually fell under the auspices of the Department of Energy, which would have subsequently made those records public as part of its declassification and public information activities.

An Extraterrestrial Craft

This was the question that was on everyone's mind, and it was the reason the report had been generated in the first place. The report contends that what crashed was not an extraterrestrial craft, despite the fact that my father's and my testimony does not support such a contention, and that evidence evaluated by a number of credible sources serves to refute such a conclusion. Unfortunately, the government chose to edit out any evidence that did not support its desired conclusion, and acknowledges only evidence and statements that fit within the report's intended premise.

The biggest question in my mind, after all these years, is this: Why did the government feel the need to perpetuate a cover-up that was foolish at its inception, and only grew more ludicrous in the successive decades? Why was the government willing to allow the reputation of my father, a man who had served with devotion and honor, to be attacked—and even destroyed—rather than acknowledge a 60-year-old lie?

This, for me, is the bitter part of the Roswell legacy. But there is so much more to the story. Before we go any further, however, I think it is only appropriate to take a closer look at those Mogul balloons. After all, where the Roswell Incident is concerned, Mogul balloons are the government's story, and it's sticking to it. Let's poke a few more holes in that story.

CHAPTER 4
What Was a Mogul Balloon?

The Japanese formally surrendered on September 2, 1945, and the United States was entering a period in which surveillance of our enemies had become an imperative in the effort to establish and maintain world peace. As is typical during wartime, the technology of battle and intelligence-gathering had advanced at breakneck speed. In the late 1930s, Dr. Maurice Ewing of Columbia University had experimented with the theory of a "sound channel" that exists underwater, where sound vibrations or waves could be transferred distances of thousands of miles without enough degradation to disrupt the signal. His theory was later applied to sound channels high in the stratosphere. It was from these experiments that Project Mogul was born in 1945, at the onset of the Cold War.

A portion of a Mogul balloon.

The project's premise was quite simple: to suspend a microphone high up in the stratosphere using a string of neoprene weather balloons. The microphone would be capable of detecting long-range sound transmissions created by the Soviet Union. If the Soviets tested a nuclear bomb or set off a missile, the sound waves created could be detected and deciphered though the Mogul program.

The Project Mogul device consisted of three components: (1) An expendable microphone for sound wave detection, (2) A transmitter used to send the information picked up by the microphones to the receiver on the ground or in the air, and (3) A balloon train and ballast to lift the devices. Rawin radar targets were also used to track the device.

Under the direction of Dr. Charles Moore, the balloon transport system for the Mogul device was designed and constructed for the military by the New York University (NYU) "balloon group," in charge of testing the constant-level balloon system, and Columbia University, responsible for the acoustical equipment. In keeping with the Army's protocol for highly classified projects, each group was aware of only that portion of the project that was directly affected by their respective area of expertise, and remained in the dark as to the nature of the project as a whole. Between September 30, 1946, and December 31, 1950, the Research Division of the College of Engineering of NYU conducted research on controllable ascent balloon transport systems under contract for the Army, unaware of the final application intended. As a matter of fact, Dr. Moore did not learn the details—or even the existence—of Project Mogul until UFO researcher Robert Todd told him about it in 1992.

The detection/transmitter package was carried aloft by spherically shaped balloons, much like the early example in the included picture. The balloons were made of a film of natural or synthetic rubber (neoprene), at a standardized weight of 350 grams. Before launch, a neoprene balloon was inflated with lighter-than-air gas, typically helium, to a diameter of approximately 6 feet (2 meters). This size provided sufficient lift to carry a radiosonde payload of several pounds. The thickness of the balloon's skin ranged from 2/1000 to 4/1000 of an inch at the time of inflation, but as the balloon ascended to an altitude of approximately 25 miles, it stretched to a mere 1/10,000 of an inch thick, its diameter swelling from its initial 6 feet to a diameter of between 24 and 32 feet—whereupon the neoprene ruptured and the balloon burst.

An integral part of the detection equipment was a radiosonde (Rawinsonde or radio wind sonde) package with an attached radar reflector that would determine wind direction and speed at various altitudes during the ascent of the package. The reflector was utilized to track the Mogul device and sonobuoy. In several of the flights, corner reflectors called Rawin targets were used in place of the radiosonde (see description on the following page). The components of the radiosonde device were contained in a robust, lightweight, white cardboard (or plastic) instrument package, approximately the size of a large shoe box.

The sonobuoy was a large cylindrical object, nearly 3 feet long and 4 3/4 inches wide and weighing 17 1/2 pounds. If a radiosonde was being used, a system of bellows expanded and contracted depending upon the altitude of the balloon chain, and would release ballast at predetermined altitudes. If there was no radiosonde, the ballast would simply dribble off fluid as time passed. Connected to the radiosonde box were a series of parachutes that would return the instrument packages safely to Earth.

Corner reflectors or Rawin targets were used in place of the radiosonde to track the balloon trains from either the air or ground. The Rawin targets were composed of a paper-backed tinfoil, and resembled a box kite constructed of balsa wood sticks and metalized paper, similar to a candy bar wrapper, taped to hold the foil to the sticks. Several of these were attached in the theory that radar detection would be easier if there were several targets, rather than just one.

As noted earlier, Army Air Force records indicate that there were a total of 11 balloon flights attempted by researchers from New York University in all of 1947. If you recall, when explaining the Roswell Incident, the government's story focused mainly upon Flight #4, which was launched June 3. Yet Flight #10 was the only one whose actual path came even remotely close to the site, and that flight was later seen still aloft, far to the north over Colorado.

According to the New York University balloon group records, Flight #4 contained the following items:

➢ 28 neoprene balloons
➢ Sonobuoy microphone, dry cell batteries, and an FM transmitter
➢ 4 Rawin radar targets, composed of balsa sticks and metalized paper
➢ Multiple plastic tubes containing a liquid ballast dribbler system
➢ 3 silk canopy parachutes (highly visible colors)
➢ 600-plus feet of braided nylon cord

On Flight #4, there was no radiosonde for tracking, as it had been replaced with the four radar targets.

The items listed here were used in a great number of different research programs, and anyone with even the most rudimentary knowledge of weather balloons and radar targets would have been able to identify them. When rancher Mac Brazel originally brought the material into the police station, even the sheriff—untrained though he was in the radar technology of the time—would have been able to recognize the material as components of a weather balloon. If the government's published accounts were true, and the debris Brazel found actually *was* from a weather or Mogul balloon, the story would likely have ended right there.

When my father investigated the crash site, he ascertained the types of debris and the size of the crash site. He never mentioned seeing any electronic components such as the sonobuoy microphone, batteries, or other items such as parachutes or rope that would have been part of a weather balloon or Mogul device. The foil debris that we looked at on our kitchen floor was not paper that had been metalized on one side. The beams that I saw and handled were made of some kind of metal, definitely not balsa wood. Even as a child, I could easily tell the difference.

The size of the debris field and the amount of debris at the crash site deviated so dramatically from the government's story that it would have taken a simultaneous crash of every Mogul balloon ever constructed—many times over—at this exact spot to even come close to the mass of debris my father saw.

Although the government reported that it was Mogul balloon Flight #4 and its radar targets that were found at the debris site, the balloon group at New York University commented that it was more likely that Flight #11 would have landed on the Foster Ranch instead. However, Flight #11 had no Rawin targets whatsoever. I once had a discussion with Professor Moore (which I'll go into more detail about in the next chapter), and he commented that Flight #4's radiosonde had a cardboard housing. I later found out that Flight #11 had a radiosonde, but Flight #4 did not. In a way, Dr. Moore confirmed that the balloon in the government's cover-up was from another flight, and not #4. Thus, I believe that we can discount the validity of the staged photos of my father holding a Rawin target, because there were none on the lost Mogul balloon flight anyway.

Let's take a closer look at Flight #11. Its telemetry failed over Arabela, New Mexico, where all tracking was terminated. If you compare its flight path to the trajectory of Flight #10, which was more fully documented (yet probably quite similar to that of Flight #11), the balloon would have continued heading north past Albuquerque and Pueblo, Colorado. Because the telemetry of Flight #11 failed, however, everything after Arabela is simply a guess. Even so, the wind patterns in the stratosphere where these balloons travel are typically quite consistent, and their direction changes slowly, so the trajectory of the Mogul flights should have been similar.

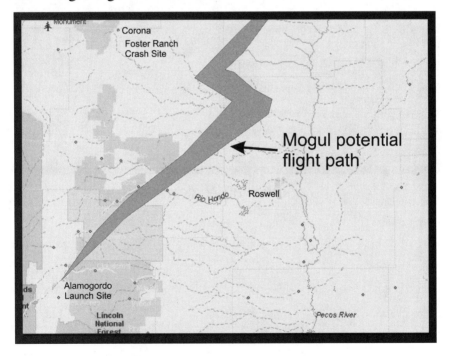

Flight path of the Mogul balloon.

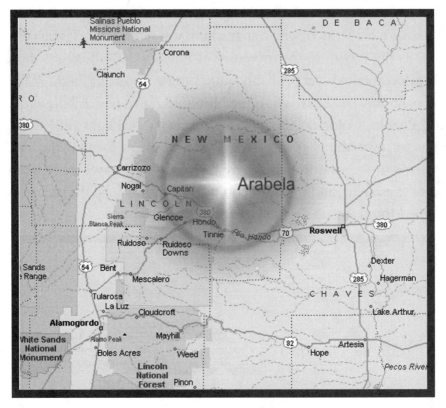

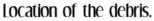

Location of the debris.

CHAPTER 5
Dr. Moore: Mogul
Balloon Scientist

The year 1997 was a special one, being the 50th anniversary of the Roswell event. My wife, Linda, and I, along with our two youngest daughters, Marissa and Mackenzie, made plans to go down to the "festival" that was being held to commemorate the event. As had happened on many other occasions, I received a phone call in which the person on the other line apparently knew of my plans almost before I did. The person requested that I stay over in Socorro, New Mexico, on the way to Roswell. Apparently there was a gentleman there who needed to talk to me.

We booked a room in Socorro and continued with our plans. Shortly after we arrived at our motel, there was a knock on our door. As it turned out, our visitor was none other than Dr. Charles Moore, who had been the head of the NYU balloon portion of Project Mogul. Our meeting was a pleasant one, and Dr. Moore, a gentleman in every sense of the word, told me that he had in his possession a Rawin target, and that he wanted me to look it over and tell him what I thought. In particular, he was interested in having me compare it to what I had seen in my kitchen in Roswell 50 years before. (There is a photograph of Dr. Moore holding a Rawin target; it was not taken at our meeting, but it shows Dr. Moore holding a target similar to that one.)

The target he showed me had the appearance of a box kite, quite similar to those I might have made as a child. The actual construction was quite simple: There was a framework of balsa wood sticks, taped to a white paper body that was coated on one side with some kind of metallic coating, like the wrapper on a chocolate bar. It was all pretty much identical to the material in the old photo taken of my father holding one of these targets. Let's take a closer look at the components of the target.

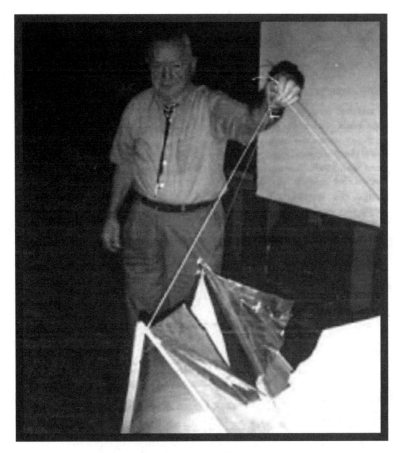

Dr. Moore holding a radar target array.

The Tape

As Dr. Moore and I were discussing the difference between the debris I had seen and the target he was holding, he commented that the tape on the original targets had been decorated with flowers and berries in a Christmas motif, rather than being clear, as it was on the one he currently held. (More than three years previously, he had told Air Force investigators that the reflectors had been manufactured by a New York toy company, which had reinforced the seams with leftover tape that had "pinkish-purple, abstract, flower-like designs." He and others have surmised that this was what my dad and I could have interpreted as hieroglyphics.)

In any event, the differences between the target Dr. Moore brought to our meeting and the materials I had seen in my kitchen 50 years prior were quite obvious. As I had noted earlier, the "foil" in the debris my father showed us was quite different from the paper-backed foil of the radar target. Neither the foil nor the tape I was shown resembled those in the original debris. Following is a reproduction of Dr. Moore's drawings of the symbols on the tape.

Drawing of symbols by Dr. Moore.

His symbols are just outlines, and the originals are at least an inch high. The symbols I viewed on the I-beams were solid figures of a purple/violet hue, with no distinctive outline. In fact, the symbols were so subtle that I didn't even notice them until direct light reflected off of them. They were clearly not line drawings, and were less than 3/8 of an inch in height. I had a facsimile made to better demonstrate the actual appearance of the beams.

Later on, my daughter Denice did some research on tapes manufactured during that time period that had been printed with a Christmas motif. She was lucky enough to locate and purchase some from a collector. Unfortunately, those samples have been misplaced through the years, and did not resemble the designs on the I-beams my father and I saw anyway.

When Dr. Moore was subsequently interviewed by NBC for a program about Roswell, he described the symbols on the tape not as flowers, but as mathematical symbols or Greek letters. I have to wonder, why the change? The symbols I had seen on the debris were not printed on tape, nor were they holiday floral or berry designs, as Dr. Moore had initially described them. Neither were they Greek letters or mathematical symbols; they were, instead, geometric symbols. As much as I respect Dr. Moore, I have to wonder at the changes in his story. My assumption is that he revised his comments to more accurately match my own recollection of the debris I had examined with my father, rather than to describe what was actually on the tape. I would prefer to give him the benefit of the doubt and assume that he really does not remember what the tape on the original targets looked like.

My regard for Dr. Moore aside, I find myself unsure as to whether the flowered tape actually existed on the materials shown to photographers. In all of the photographs of the Rawin targets that were used in Project Mogul, not one of them shows anything resembling the decorative tape he has described.

The picture of Dr. Moore shows one of the ML-307 Rawin radar targets used in Mogul flights. Though it is difficult to see due to the age and poor quality of the photograph, there is no flowered tape, and the white strip is the paper backing folded over one of the structural members. If you look closely, you can even make out the buttons on his shirt, so you would think there should be some evidence of flowers along the taped edge if they were there.

One would also think that, as well-documented and -photographed as the Mogul tests were, some photographs should exist that show the decorative tape described in the government's story, but no such photographs have ever been made public. This is just another example of how the Mogul balloon didn't fit the description of what my father and I saw, and how, in my opinion, truth has been supplanted with disinformation.

I realize that it might seem that I am belaboring the significance of the tape—or, rather, the lack of the tape—but the official story has relied so heavily upon this as a plausible explanation for the symbols that adorned the I-beams in the original debris, that I feel it represents a significant flaw in what I firmly believe to be the government's cover-up.

The Paper

As I have noted previously, the foil in the debris my father showed me was very similar in appearance to modern-day heavy-duty aluminum foil, except that it was much lighter, and had a dull, burnished appearance, rather than the highly reflective finish of aluminum foil. As I also noted earlier, the material on the Rawin target Dr. Moore showed me had an appearance very similar to that of a candy bar wrapper—shiny on one side, and paper on the other. I asked Dr. Moore if any of the radar targets they had used had been foil without the paper backing. He responded that all of the targets used in the Mogul device used paper-backed foil, but that he thought the Navy may have used foil without the paper backing in their radar targets. Such foil, however, would not possess the resiliency and strength of the foil I had handled in the original debris.

The Balsa Wood Sticks

The wood sticks that made up the structure of the Rawin target were obviously lightweight balsa wood, quite fragile, and identical to what I used in building stick models as a child. The I-beams I examined in the wreckage, however, were made of some lightweight metal that had an appearance similar to titanium. My father had, on numerous occasions, made note of the fact that these members were unbelievably strong—strong enough that even a sledge hammer would not dent them. If you were to take a sledge hammer to one of the balsa wood sticks used on the Rawin targets, all you would end up with is a handful of shattered splinters.

Electronic Components

During our conversation, I asked Dr. Moore if any of the electronic components in the Rawin or Mogul devices had been housed in black plastic similar to the material I had seen in the debris. He responded that the radiosonde devices that contained the electronic components were housed in cardboard boxes, rather than plastic. I asked him for his explanation of the fact that there were no electronic components in the debris, because if what we had examined had been sonobuoys or radiosondes, as he claimed, components such as transmitters and batteries would have been found somewhere in or around the crash site. I also asked him to explain why no weather balloons were found in the wreckage, when each of the flights he had conducted had been carried aloft by such balloons, and at least some remnants of the balloon material should have remained with the other material. He admitted that he could offer no explanation for either discrepancy.

In the end, we parted with a handshake. Though Dr. Moore had done his best to convince me that what I had seen had been a Mogul balloon, I think he realized that my description, which had never changed, was not going to change then either.

The conversation with Dr. Moore only served to further convince me that what my father had brought into our kitchen that night had not been a Mogul device. The discrepancies between what I had seen in Roswell and a Rawin radar target were too numerous, and too clear. Dr. Moore, however, remained convinced that what I saw was a radar target, and assumed that I was mistaken in my memories of what I had seen. I am just as convinced that what I saw was not part of a radar target, nor could any of the debris I saw and handled have come from a Mogul device. I know what I saw, and I know that there are people within the government who know as well, but who remain in the shadows. It is perhaps these people about whom I was cautioned when asked if I had ever gotten any threatening phone calls (I'll go into this in the next chapter).

A few years before I had my meeting with Dr. Moore, I received a call from the Air Force. Because I was a colonel in the Montana National Guard, he began the conversation with, "Colonel, we need your help." I was not sure at first who it was that needed my help. As it turned out, the Air Force wanted to feel me out as to what I thought the debris from Roswell really was. I began by describing what I had seen, in as much detail as my memory would allow. At the end of my description, the caller said that he believed that I had seen parts of a Mogul balloon device, namely the radar reflector that was a part of the Mogul balloon train. I then pointed out the discrepancies between what I had seen and handled in Roswell and the radar target. He was not impressed. I then asked him, just as I would later ask Dr. Moore, if the plastic Bakelite-esque material I had felt could have been part of the housing for the radio transmitter carried aloft with the radar targets. He said that he did not think so, because the radio was housed in either a cardboard or aluminum container. As we reached the end of our conversation, he said something to the effect that he was not sure what I had seen, but that it had obviously not been part of the Mogul project.

I later learned that he had been tasked with gathering pertinent information for inclusion in the official Air Force document I mentioned previously, *The Roswell Report: Case Closed*. When that document was published, it concluded that what my father and I had seen had indeed been a radar target. Inasmuch as the points made in my conversation with the Air Force were contrary to such a conclusion—I'd held firmly to my opinion that it was *not* a radar target, and the Air Force official had admitted he couldn't say for sure what I had seen—I realized, once and for all, that the government was either too inept to relay a factual account, or was participating in a well-choreographed cover-up.

As did my late father, I have no doubt that what I saw in Roswell was unearthly in origin. The only questions that continue to nag at me are, first of all: from where did it come? Secondly, what does the government I have joyfully served for all these years have to gain from hiding the truth? And lastly—though just as worrisome as the other questions—to what lengths will it go to perpetuate the falsehood?

CHAPTER 6
A Government Official's Admission

I t was a bright summer day in the early 1990s, and I had just re-turned home from my annual two-week training session for the Montana National Guard. To say that it had been a grueling two weeks would be a gross understatement. Between routine medical duties and the constant helicopter support training sessions, it was much more stressful than the time spent in our civilian occupations, and I was looking forward to returning home and taking it easy for a while.

When I got home, I found in my accumulated mail an invitation to a UFO conference in Washington, D.C. The meeting was funded by an anonymous host, who invited me—along with my family—to attend, with all our expenses paid. It sounded like a great deal to me, so I talked to my wife, Linda, about it. Even though she has always been less trusting than I am, I was surprised when she insisted that, because I didn't know who our "benefactor" was, she wouldn't allow the family to go. It seems that before—and especially during—my absence, we had been getting numerous phone calls from people who would not identify themselves, but would inquire as to my where-abouts, then abruptly hang up. Linda was actually concerned that if we all went to Washington, we would perhaps never be seen again. As I recall, she said something to the effect that all of us would be "thrown in the Potomac." The bottom line is that she was too worried and protective of our family to let the kids go. I thought she might have been overreacting a bit, but because she is normally a level-headed person, I had to respect her feelings. After giving it some thought, I told her that I felt it would be a good idea for me to go, but I would do so by myself.

Not too long after I accepted my invitation, my secretary, Linda Story, received a phone call from someone who would not reveal his identity, but claimed that he needed to speak with me. She told the caller that I was seeing a patient at the moment, and asked that he call back a bit later. The caller informed her that he was from Washington, and that it was imperative that he speak with me *immediately*. Apparently something in his words or tone convinced my secretary that the call was important enough to warrant interrupting me, so she put the caller on hold to inform me of the apparently urgent nature of the call.

I excused myself, went into my office, and picked up the phone. The caller still would not identify himself, but said he knew of my meeting in Washington and wanted to talk to me when I got there. He gave me a Capitol Building address at which to meet him, which I found somehow reassuring. I didn't really think that I was likely to be kidnapped by someone in the government. In hindsight, perhaps my sense of security wasn't well-founded, and I should not have felt so reassured. After all, this unknown government official had been tracking my whereabouts enough to know that I had been invited to a meeting on UFOs, and had obviously known when and where.

Upon my arrival at my hotel in Washington, there was a message waiting for me from this same official. I couldn't help but wonder how he knew where I would be staying, almost before I knew myself. The message simply stated that he wanted to visit with me at the Capitol Building the following morning. Had I been an avid reader of intrigue novels, I would probably have been more alarmed than curious at his resourcefulness. As it was, I found it quite enticing that somebody would put such effort into contacting me.

After reading the message, I went to my room to prepare for the meeting. At the meeting, I was going around chatting with people and introducing myself when an individual approached me and said there was someone who wanted to talk to me. He took me gently by the arm and guided me across the crowded room. I was introduced to a gentleman who was quite tall, and of central European descent. His name was Hans-Adam II of Lichtenstein. He asked me a few questions about Roswell, and after we had spoken for a few minutes, we went our separate ways to mingle among the other attendees. My impression of the party was that it had been interesting, and filled with an amenable group of people, but that it had not been particularly memorable. It was only later that I found out the gentleman who had sought me out was the party's host, the Prince of Lichtenstein. I reminded myself then that I needed to reevaluate my definition of the word *memorable*.

The next morning, I went to the Capitol Building to meet with the mysterious government official. I was greeted by security, which checked and found my name on the appointment list. I was shown to an office, where I was left to sit in the outer lobby to await my meeting. As I sat there waiting, I remember feeling somewhat antsy, because my flight back home was going to be leaving later that afternoon, and I didn't want to miss it.

After a few minutes, the government official emerged from his office and approached me, smiling and extending his hand. Nothing in particular about him stood out. He was the kind of person you would see on the street and never give another thought to—average height and weight, and friendly. He did not, however, waste any time with small talk, beyond a perfunctory, if seemingly warm, greeting. His demeanor stiffened a bit, and he actually kind of blurted out, "I understand that you saw…at Roswell. Could we talk about it? Do we need to go to a secure room?"

I was put at ease with his friendly informality, as well as the implicit intrigue in his last question, but told him, "No, I have nothing to say that I haven't said before." He responded that *he* might have things to tell *me* that would require a secure room, and suggested that I follow him. We proceeded down a corridor that ended at an elevator that brought us deep underground. As we descended into the depths of the building, my wife's concerns came to the forefront of my mind, and I thought to myself that I might never see the light of day again. When the doors opened, we emerged into what appeared to be a basement area with concrete walls, steam piping, and corridors branching off from the one in which we stood.

The official led me down a passageway to a doorway that led to a fancy paneled meeting room, similar to the main conference room one would find in any large company—save for the fact that there were no windows, as this room was deep underground. Inside the room was a long table with perhaps 30 chairs. On the walls above the table were pictures of the country's founding fathers. The overall impression I got was that this was a room used for private meetings of powerful people.

My host closed the door behind me and sat at the head of the table. In front of him was a yellow legal pad and a copy of a book titled *Majestic*, by Whitley Strieber, for which I had written the foreword. He pointed to the book and stated, "This is not fiction." Although the book is a fictionalized story of the Roswell Incident, my host made it clear that he believed that the story of a UFO crash in Roswell was, indeed, a fact.

He asked me to describe what I had seen in my family's kitchen that night so many years before. I closed my eyes for a moment, recalling that night as if it had happened a few nights before, rather than the decades that had passed. As I began to tell my story, my mind was filled with the minutest of details; the sounds, the textures, and weight of the items I had held, and even the strange symbols that had adorned the pieces of I-beam.

He asked me where I thought the debris might be now, and I responded, "Don't you know? You guys are the ones that have it." I commented that I had often wondered about the "Blue Room" at Wright-Patterson Air Force Base that Barry Goldwater had mentioned in his writings, but had never been allowed to actually visit. (I'll discuss this in more detail in a little while.) My host answered that he did not know where the debris was.

I asked him if he had seen the movie *Raiders of the Lost Ark*, and he responded that he had. I asked if he remembered the last scene, in which a person is seen pushing a huge crate containing the Ark down the row of a giant warehouse, packed floor to ceiling with thousands upon thousands of similar-looking crates. He nodded his acknowledgment. I said, "Perhaps *that's* where it is." He laughed, and said I was probably right.

At the end of our discussion, I told him that I had one question for him. I asked him when he thought the government would release the truth about UFOs, specifically about the Roswell Incident. He said that, honestly, if it were up to him, the veil of secrecy would have been lifted years ago. But, he added, it was unfortunately *not* up to him.

He told me that he had been charged with the responsibility of investigating the operation of a "black government" within the government, where funds were being spent without appropriate oversight to maintain a false story about the Roswell Incident and cover the true story up. He said that his job was to report to the Senate Appropriations Committee, and advise them as to where these tax dollars were going, and why.

I have to admit that I was pretty well stunned by his response. I had long known that there was a concerted effort on the part of the government to hide the truth of what had happened in July of 1947, but here was a *government official* standing right there in front of me, in a room reserved for secure government meetings, telling me that my suspicions were valid, and the cover-up real.

He then asked me whether I had received any threatening phone calls. I told him about the anonymous hang-up calls, but assured him that none had gone so far as to actually threaten us. He then ripped off the top page of his legal pad, wrote down all of his contact information, and handed the paper to me, telling me that if I ever was threatened, I was to contact him immediately. To this day, I have kept that piece of paper, and have even stored a copy of the information in a safe place, should the need for it ever arise. I have never divulged the official's name to anyone, in keeping with the discretion he requested of—and offered to—me at our meeting.

Our conversation then diverted to more mundane subjects as he led me from the conference room, back to the elevator, and finally out to the main lobby. He reiterated his instructions to call him if the situation we had discussed came to pass, and then he bid me farewell. We parted company, and I found that I had a great deal to think about on my way to the airport and on the flight home.

I feel pretty certain that the debris remains in the control of the so-called black government, and am equally certain that it has been thoroughly researched, possibly offering up some technological insights that were heretofore unknown. As far as I know, this meeting was the first and only time that anyone associated with the government had tacitly admitted that the Roswell event was, as my father and I had long known, the crash of a machine from another planet.

The Black Government

Ever since I spoke with that official back in the early 1990s, I have come to believe that the black government he spoke about is something more than the fabrication of wild-eyed conspiracy theorists. So I ask you to please hear me out before you banish me to the tinfoil hat crowd. The black government consists of a specialized, unelected group of officials. They apparently have billions of dollars at their disposal to protect the rest of the government and the people from information that they consider to be in some way harmful or dangerous to our way of life. Their access to tax dollars is through other programs that either exist only on paper, or whose accounting methods allow them to accumulate funds covertly, without the encumbrance of a paper trail subject to any kind of oversight.

In the movies, the members of this shadow organization have been fictionalized as the "Men In Black," clearly a case of art imitating life. It is in cases such as this that the line between science fiction and science fact is quite blurred. Although some members of our elected government—such as the official with whom I met—know about the black government, they discuss its existence very discreetly, if at all, knowing that if all evidence of an extraterrestrial visitation can be made to disappear, the elimination of an overly talkative government employee would be child's play.

Earlier in this chapter, I referred to government officials such as Barry Goldwater, who were aware of—but not allowed to see—the area where I suspect the Roswell debris was hidden away. On these pages, I have reproduced a couple of documents that I feel add some credence to my suspicion that the Roswell debris is located at Wright-Patterson Air Force Base, near Dayton, Ohio.

Given the fact that I was informed by an obviously highly placed government official that my interpretation of the Roswell event is not fiction, and that there is an arm of the government that is neither elected by, nor accountable to the taxpayer, and which has at its disposal huge sums of money being spent illegally to keep events such as the Roswell story hidden from the public, I have to ask myself why.

Does the government fear that allowing the public to know there are extraterrestrial civilizations would result in widespread panic? Would our sense of security be so challenged by the knowledge that those civilizations might be significantly more advanced than we are technologically, that our very society would be shaken as a result? Perhaps the government feels it cannot allow its citizens to even consider the possibility that we are not in control of our skies, and that our continued existence depends upon the good will of someone about whom we know virtually nothing. A frightening possibility, perhaps, if one is prone to fearfulness rather than common sense.

My feeling is that a race (for lack of a better word) sufficiently advanced to be able to traverse the cosmos to visit us does not mean harm to us. After all, if they are that technologically advanced and wanted to harm us, it is doubtful that we would still be alive to worry about it. One thing that does concern me is that there may be many different civilizations out there capable of interstellar travel, and it may be our good fortune that the ones who have approached us thus far are benevolent in their intentions. Suppose, however, that there are civilizations out there whose intentions are less than benevolent, or who view us as so inferior as to be unworthy of their regard, who look upon us in much the same way as we look upon insects or rodents. God help us if one of those more malevolent types were to come calling. I, for one, would prefer to acknowledge and ultimately establish a positive relationship with the "good guys," whose friendship might prove invaluable to us, both as teachers and allies, should we face the unthinkable prospect of an attack from outside our little realm.

Ultimately, the only way we can hope to develop a friendly relationship with any peoples—be they from our own world or beyond—is by facing the truth, by learning all that we can about them, rather than hiding ourselves from their very existence. This is yet another case in which the decision to live in and act out of fear has the potential to cause that fear to come to fruition. We deserve better than that, and our government owes it to us to treat us as citizens, rather than as children.

CHAPTER 7
Other Visits

For me, a big part of the Roswell legacy, beyond its effect on the Marcel family, has been an abiding interest in ufology and space travel. These topics fascinate me. And although I don't want to stray too far off course, I think it appropriate at this point to briefly explore well-documented events that, although not directly related to Roswell, bolster the case of Roswell and UFO "believers." In this chapter, we'll look at a couple of unexplained UFO events that particularly interest me.

Throughout the years I have studied a lot of so-called UFO incidents, and many have turned out to have earthly explanations—much to the disappointment, I'm sure, of some UFO enthusiasts. A few of these incidents, however, remain mysteries, and they are mysteries about which the government has been less than forthcoming. Take, for example, some of the strange goings-on in my home state of Montana.

As I will discuss later, perhaps our government has worked so diligently to hide the truth about the Roswell crash to protect us from the fact that the military is not as invincible as it would have us believe. How safe would the American people feel if they knew that there existed a potential enemy that had the capability of getting past all our strategic defenses at will? Ironically, the Roswell Incident was far from the first—and certainly not the last—event to demonstrate just that. Furthermore, there have been incidents in more recent years that leave us to wonder whether the "visitors" necessarily hold to some noble principle such as the "Prime Directive" so often recited in the Star Trek franchise, which forbade influencing the internal affairs of other civilizations. Although *Star Trek* is of course fiction, one would hope that real-life interstellar travelers would have some sort of code that included a policy of noninterference. But maybe that's just wishful thinking on our part. (To tell the truth, I'm not so sure that humans would be able to avoid interfering if it suited their fancy; we don't seem to be very good about practicing our own finest principles.) At any rate, there are a couple of specific UFO instances that have never been properly explained by officials, and that could certainly be construed as evidence of extraterrestrial intervention in human activities. In these cases it was much to the chagrin of the people directly involved—most notably the military. If you're a skeptic, indulge me for a few moments while we look at a couple of incidents in which it seems that extraterrestrials (or *something*) actually demonstrated that they/it had the means to inhibit our ability to kill each other—essentially rendering the military irrelevant.

The area around Great Falls, Montana, has had a high occurrence of UFO sightings since the 1950s. However, what happened on March 16, 1967, near Malmstrom Air Force Base, just outside Great Falls, went pretty far beyond a mere sighting. On that morning, Crew Commander Captain Eric Carlson and Deputy Crew Commander First Lieutenant Walt Figel, the Echo Flight (E-Flight) Missile Combat Crew near Malmstrom Air Force Base, were below ground in the silo, in the E-Flight Launch Control Center. Missile maintenance crews and security teams had remained at two of the launch facilities after working there the previous day. During the early morning hours, the crews reported that they had seen several glowing, disc-shaped UFOs. Some of them were pretty disturbed by these sightings; one security policeman was reportedly so affected by this incident that he never returned to missile security duty.

Around 8:30 that morning, the alarm horn sounded, indicating that one of the Minuteman Intercontinental Ballistic Missiles (ICBMs), under the supervision of Figel and Carlson, had gone off alert, which meant it had become inoperable. Figel became understandably upset, figuring that the maintenance personnel had failed to notify him that maintenance work was being performed on a missile, necessitating putting it on "off-alert" status. Because such notification is required by very rigid procedure—after all, these were nuclear weapons—Figel immediately called the missile site, ready to give somebody a serious butt chewing.

When Figel spoke with the on-site security guard, however, he learned that no maintenance work had been performed that morning. The guard also informed Figel that a UFO had been observed hovering directly over the site. At first, Figel thought that the guard must have been putting something in his thermos besides coffee...until one by one, across the board, the other missiles also started to go off alert in rapid succession. Within seconds, the entire flight of 10 ICBMs was down, all indicating a "No Go" condition. When the trouble-shooting procedure checklist had been completed for each missile site, it was discovered that the missiles had gone off alert status due to a Guidance and Control System fault, which typically occurs only after a loss of main and backup power. The troubleshooting checklist showed that there had been no such interruption of power to the sites, and that the missiles' guidance and control systems had simply—and inexplicably—malfunctioned. Figel ordered two of the Echo Security Alert Teams (SATs) to those sites where the maintenance crews were present, but did not inform the teams of the reports about the UFO sighting. On arrival at the launch facilities, the SATs reported back that all of the maintenance and security personnel present at each site reported seeing UFOs hovering over each of the two sites.

When Captain Don Crawford and his crew relieved the Echo Flight crew later that morning, Crawford noted that both Carlson and Figel were still visibly shaken. Crawford also recalled that the maintenance crews worked on the missiles the entire day and late into the night during his shift to bring the missiles back to ready condition. The end result was that a full complement of missiles—crucial elements in the country's deterrent forces—had been out of service for an entire day. Obviously, when such a significant and rare event occurs, all hell breaks loose, and anyone bearing any responsibility for the malfunction faces, at best, a reprimand, and at worst, severe disciplinary action. But after an extensive investigation by both Boeing (the chief contractor) and the military, there was no reasonable explanation for the event, much less a finding of culpability on the part of on-duty personnel.

Before dawn on that same morning, a similar—but even more ominous—sequence of events occurred about 20 miles southeast, near the town of Roy, Montana, at the Oscar Flight Launch Control Center. According to Deputy Missile Combat Crew Commander Robert Salas, who was at the Oscar Flight Control Center that morning, it had been a clear, cold night. On-duty airmen often looked to the sky to observe shooting stars, but what one airman saw that morning seemed to be something else entirely. He observed what he first assumed to be a star, until it began to move erratically across the sky; shortly afterward, he saw another light do the same thing. This time, however, it was much larger and closer than the first. The airman asked his flight security controller to come and take a look. The two men stood there watching as the lights streaked directly above them, then stopped, changed directions at high speed, and returned to their positions overhead. The flight security controller ran into the building and phoned Salas at his station in the silo, reporting what they had seen, and stressing that they weren't aircraft. Salas initially figured the men, who were conscientious in their service but not above a bit of harmless kidding around, were doing just that. His response was, "Great. You just keep watching them and let me know if they get any closer." He then directed the security controller to report back if anything more significant happened.

Even though his response was not indicative of any particular concern, Salas knew that this kind of behavior was out of character for on-duty air security personnel, who were typically very professional, especially when addressing a superior.

A few minutes later, the security controller called again, this time obviously agitated. The man literally shouted, "Sir, there's one hovering outside the front gate!"

Salas, somewhat unnerved at this point, retorted, "One *what*?"

"A UFO! It's just sitting there. We're all just looking at it. What do you want us to do?"

Salas asked for a description, but the security controller couldn't describe it, other than to say that it was glowing red. "What are we supposed to do?" he asked Salas.

"Make sure the site is secure and I'll phone the command post," Salas told him. He was a bit taken aback when the security controller said, "Sir, I have to go now. One of the guys just got injured."

Before Salas could inquire as to the nature of the man's injury, the security controller terminated the call. Salas immediately went to the quarters of his commander, Lieutenant Fred Meiwald, awakened him, and began to brief him about the phone calls and the events that were transpiring topside. In the middle of this conversation, the first alarm horn was activated, and Salas and Meiwald immediately looked at the panel of indicator lights at the commander's station. A "No Go" light and two red security lights were lit, indicating problems at one of the missile sites. Meiwald jumped up to query the system in order to determine the cause of the problem, but before he could complete that task, several other alarms went off at other sites simultaneously. Within the next few seconds, six to eight missiles had spontaneously become inoperable.

After reporting this incident to the command post, Salas phoned the security controller, who told him that the man who had approached the UFO had not been seriously injured, but was being evacuated by helicopter to the base. Once topside, Salas spoke directly with the security guard, who repeated that the UFO had a red glow, adding that it appeared to be saucer-shaped. He also repeated that it had been hovering silently just outside the front gate. Salas sent a security patrol to check the launch facilities after the shutdown, and they reported sighting another UFO, and then immediately lost radio contact with him. When Salas and his crew were relieved by the next shift later that morning, the missiles had still not been brought online.

Despite extensive efforts by both on-site technicians and Boeing engineers, no cause for the shutdowns was ever found. According to Boeing engineering team leader Robert Kaminski, "There were no significant failures, engineering data, or findings that would explain how 10 missiles were knocked off alert." He added that there was no technical explanation that could explain the event. The systems could be taken off-line via the introduction of a pulse of electric current directly at the computer controller, but the only way a pulse or noise could be sent in from outside the shielded system was through an electromagnetic pulse (EMP) from an unknown source. Such pulses typically occur immediately after the detonation of a nuclear device in the general area, but no such detonation had occurred. Other sources of EMPs at that time would have involved the use of huge pieces of specialized equipment, none of which was present at the site. There was also some speculation that the events could have been caused by a massive power failure, but according to William Dutton, another Boeing engineer who investigated this as a possible explanation, there were no such power anomalies in the area. A pulse of some sort caused those missile shutdowns, but the source of that pulse is still a mystery.

Late in 1975, UFOs returned to the area around Malmstrom Air Force Base. Once again they repeatedly hovered over and interfered with ICBM facilities. Though these incidents continued throughout the course of several months and received a lot of press coverage in Montana, they were mostly ignored by the national news media. They did, however, become the subject of a now out-of-print book, *Mystery Stalks The Prairie*, by Keith Wolverton (who at the time was deputy sheriff of Cascade County), and journalist Roberta Donovan. A series of Freedom of Information Act (FOIA) lawsuits uncovered more information, and Air Force records show that during the same period, UFO activity occurred at other military bases in the northern part of the United States. Though some folks have speculated that these events were merely elaborate Air Force tests of the security of the nation's nuclear weapons forces, military eyewitnesses and Air Force records would seem to negate that theory.

Not surprisingly, the Air Force has maintained for many years that no reported UFO incident has ever affected national security. However, considering that large numbers of Air Force personnel reported sighting UFOs at the time many of our strategic missiles became inoperable, I find it difficult to believe the Air Force's claim. I'd say it's pretty hard to ignore the national security implications of the incidents described here. In one previously classified message regarding the Echo Flight incident, SAC headquarters described it as a loss of strategic alert of all 10 missiles within 10 seconds of each other for no apparent reason, saying that the event was a "cause for grave concern."

Another even more frightening event occurred not in Montana, but in what was then the Soviet Union on October 4, 1982. In Byelokoroviche, Ukraine, where a nuclear missile launch site is located, local residents reported a large flying saucer hovering over the nearby missile silo. According to ex-KGB Colonel Igor Chernovshev, the launch crew stationed in the launch control room reported that signal lights on both control panels started to light up, indicating the missile was being prepared for a launch. This launch sequence continued for 15 seconds, stopping just before the launch would have occurred. This could have happened only on receipt of a launch code from Moscow. An investigation team analyzed the electronic complex involved, but no technical problems were discovered, and Moscow did not dispatch the launch codes.

I agree that these incidents are a cause for concern. But I also see them as yet more evidence that we are not alone. And even more than concern or fear, I find that to be a cause for great wonder.

CHAPTER 8
"Along for the Ride of My Life": Linda's Story

So far, this book has been focused upon my recollection of my own experiences, the fruits of research and interviews I've done throughout the years, and, ultimately, how being at "ground zero" of the Roswell controversy has affected my life. The story wouldn't be complete, however, if I didn't place significant emphasis upon the effects this tale has had upon my *family. I'm not so egocentric as to believe that I'm the most qualified to tell that part of the story. For that reason, I'm going to step away from the task of writing the book for a while, and let my wife, Linda, take over.*

Linda has been a real source of strength for me, supporting me when I was frustrated, sharing my tears and my laughter, and generally being the one person upon whom I could always count when life got difficult. If for no other reason than fairness, she deserves to have her say, and readers deserve to hear the voice of someone intimately involved in this whole story, yet perhaps a bit more objective than I. Besides, why should I have to do all the work to get this stuff out there for you to read? On that note, I think I'll go out and enjoy the mountain air for a while. So here is my lovely wife, Linda.

~ Jess

Well...isn't it just like Jess to drop this in my lap, so he can go out and play?! And not to even give me an easy opening line, like "Once upon a time."

To say the least, Roswell has been an adventure for me. As a small child who grew up terrified of the Northern Lights, and who became hysterical when I first saw the Russian satellite *Sputnik* in the 1950s, I think I've come a pretty long way.

My part in the Roswell story began in 1979, when I went to work as a nurse at Helena Ear, Nose, and Throat Clinic, and met Dr. Jesse Marcel. One morning over coffee, Jess's office manager made some mention of UFOs, and Jess told me that some kind of UFO had crashed outside of Roswell, New Mexico, when he was a kid. I had been exposed to stories about the missile sites outside of Great Falls, Montana, and sightings of Sasquatch. My father was a veterinarian, and was occasionally called out to investigate cattle mutilations in the area, and frequently told us stories about what he saw. So, even though the cattle-mutilation phenomenon did not become a big deal in the UFO community until many years later, I had at least a vague awareness that some strange things were happening for which nobody seemed to have a good explanation.

Even so, we hadn't actually heard anything about UFOs when I was growing up, at least not anything that made much of an impression on me. I had spent the first half of my life in rural Montana. You know, Big Sky Country, where the deer and the antelope play, and rattle-snakes hide. I think that at the time, the entire state of Montana had maybe 200,000 people. Heck, until the early 1960s, my family didn't even have a television. My first experience with anything "off-planet" was a huge country party that the people in my town threw in honor of *Sputnik*, which I not only failed to attend, but actually spent the entire time hiding in my closet, certain that it was the end of the world.

Did I, as an alleged adult, believe in UFOs? Until Jess told me his story, I hadn't ever really given them much thought, one way or another. I was just a young, single mom trying to raise three kids, and found I had little time or energy for anything besides tending to the constant flow of crises that are such an integral part of parenthood— especially *single* parenthood. Somehow, Jess's story awakened something in me; a curiosity about things I'd never considered important. About the same time, a different "curiosity" was demanding more and more of my attention. A man to whom I had deferred as a boss became my friend. A man I had liked and respected as a friend be-came more. And, after a time, I realized that I was in love with this strong, gentle man who had such interesting tales to tell. As it turned out, he was experiencing the same kind of feelings. And even though I didn't get to start my portion of this story with a "once upon a time," I have to admit that it looks as though the "happily ever after" part rings pretty true.

After a time, not only had I married my boss, but I also inherited his three kids to add to the mix with my own three. Beyond becoming mother to the Big Sky Brady Bunch, I now had to deal with something wholly alien (pun intended!) to anything in my previous experiences: UFOs.

It wasn't so difficult from a religious standpoint. I'm a Christian with a strong faith in God, but even though I had been raised to believe that humankind was God's ultimate creation, I had long thought it would be somewhat arrogant to believe that God had created life only on this planet. It was more difficult from a matter of scope. I had just never given that much thought to life beyond that which we knew and were familiar with. Even the idea of strange creatures that lived at incredible depths in the ocean seemed unreal to me. Life with Jess Marcel, however, served to broaden my horizons, and as the years went by, I found myself forced to consider new and wondrous possibilities, in a universe infinitely larger than I had ever known.

The years moved on, and we went from being the Brady Bunch to something more akin to Cheaper by the Dozen: two more kids, then grandkids. That I was busy at home was an understatement. Even that last statement was an understatement! What with my job and all the kids, I learned a new meaning for the word *frazzled*, and sometimes even wished that some alien ship would drop down and take me away somewhere quiet, if only for a day or two.

As the 50th anniversary of the Roswell crash approached in 1997, the discussion—and controversy—had again emerged, and Jess was busy doing television shows and conferences, and giving lectures on what he had seen as a young boy. After attending some of the conferences with Jess and hearing scientists, NASA employees, and individual stories told by some of the witnesses, I began to realize that this story is like a big puzzle with many pieces. It struck me that it would be awfully difficult for so many individual people from various walks of life to have manufactured this tale 60 years ago, much less sustained it all these years, without being members of a conspiracy beyond anything the fiction writers could have dreamt up. There were just too many stories—then, and in the decades since—that meshed together to complete the whole.

The one thing I had known for many years was that, as a child, Jess had seen and held pieces of what he and his father firmly believed to be part of a UFO. I was also fortunate enough to have been told the story by his dad, shortly before his death. Jesse Sr. came into the kitchen early one morning while I was fixing breakfast, sat down with a cup of coffee, and said, out of the blue, "You know, the crash at the Brazel Ranch that I investigated was not of this earth. It was scattered in a field over a large area. The rancher said his sheep wouldn't go near it. He had to take them around it for water. There were pieces of aluminum foil–like material, clear string or line that was like fishing line, and some I-beams. When you balled up the foil in your hand, it would open like it had a memory. We loaded it up into our vehicles and took it back to Roswell."

I asked him, "Did you see any little people?"

He answered, "No, just the foil and beams. It wasn't a balloon. I wouldn't have wasted my time on it if it were. It was said they found another crash site that had little people, but I never saw them. I stopped at the house on the way to the base to show Viaud and little Jess, because I knew that it was not of this earth. When word started getting out about what we found, they came out with a news report that we had found a UFO, and then they changed the story to a weather balloon."

"Did that make you mad?"

"Naw, I was military, and just doing my job."

"Didn't you think it was odd when they cleaned it up and then flew it away? Would they have done that for a weather balloon?"

"Hell, no! I was trained in this stuff, and I knew it wasn't a balloon."

I had heard this story before, of course, but it was the first time that Jesse Sr. had actually sat down and told it to me. Although he had spoken about the incident a few times to the media in recent years, he seemed to feel it was important to make a statement to me now.

Our next visit with Jesse Sr. was a sad one. It was June 1986, and Jesse Jr. had just returned from summer camp with the National Guard. I had spent two weeks in Disneyland with all of our kids and another Guard family, loaded into two vans. We had been home only a day when we got the call that Jesse Sr. was in the hospital and was not expected to live. Jesse Jr. had a private ENT practice, and had already missed two weeks of work attending Guard Camp, which was normally his "vacation." Nevertheless, we made a fast trip to Houma, Louisiana. As we'd been warned, Jess's dad died, and Jess took it awfully hard. I'd always known that Jess idolized his dad, but the sadness that hung over him really drove the point home. With the help of Jess's cousins, we packed Jesse Sr.'s house in Houma and loaded everything into a U-haul. Jess set out for the long ride back to Montana, while I flew home with his mother, Viaud.

Viaud spent the next 10 years living with us. On occasion, she would tell our friends the story of when UFO researcher Stan Friedman had come to the house in Houma in the late 1970s, and had asked Jesse Sr. about the Roswell crash. In later years, she developed Alzheimer's, and grew ever more distant from us. In spite of the challenges of caring for her, along with keeping everything else balanced on my already full plate, I am grateful for the time we had with her. One thing that still holds firm in my mind is the fact that you cannot live with someone for years, much less decades, and not know the real truth of who they are and what they say. The story I have heard from Jess, his mom, and his dad has never wavered, and even if I had never heard anyone else support the tale they told, I would know in my heart that it is true.

———————————◆———————————

Although for me the specter of Roswell had long been an accepted part of life with Jess, I think my real baptism into UFO culture occurred at a National Mutual UFO Network (MUFON) conference somewhere in the Midwest. I don't remember the exact location or date, but I certainly remember the people. I've always been a people watcher, and the conference was a real smorgasbord for me. There were people from all walks of life—educated and not-so-educated, scientists and researchers, and believers of every stripe, from new-agers to "tinfoil hats"—so I was in watcher heaven.

In October of 1988 we went to Washington D.C., where Jess was to be part of a documentary hosted by actor Mike Farrell called *UFO Cover-Up: Live!*, a two-hour prime-time syndicated television special that was broadcast in North America and elsewhere. Not being much of a television watcher, it was only after three days of rehearsal, while standing in a lunch line behind Mike, that I finally realized that he was Captain B.J. Hunnicutt from *M.A.S.H.*, the one television show I watched. When I told him that it had just dawned on me who he was, he just laughed.

People representing all the different aspects of ufology were featured in this live presentation—NASA, the CIA, and people associated with the Roswell Incident, and even the Russian government, which has publicly acknowledged several UFO sightings. In fact, this documentary was done in conjunction with the Russians via satellite. On the evening of the show, representatives from the Russian

Embassy came to watch. I was surprised to learn that the Russian government is apparently far more open in its discussion of UFOs than is our own government.

In the early 1990s, Jess was invited on an all-expense-paid trip to Washington, D.C., for a UFO conference. (He wrote about this in an earlier chapter.) Even though the kids and I had been invited as well, with all our expenses paid, we had no idea who was financing the trip. When Jess tried unsuccessfully to find out, my occasionally overactive imagination kicked in, and I let him know that I was sure we would all wind up dumped in the Potomac River, never to be seen again. Jess really wanted to go, however, so we reached a compromise. I told Jess that he could go if he really wanted to, but that the kids and I were going to stay home.

After Jess arrived, he called home and told me he was staying at the Hilton, and attending a party hosted by the Prince of Lichtenstein, who, as it turns out, was bankrolling the UFO event. Apparently, the prince was interested in UFOs, and the Roswell crash in particular. I could have kicked myself for letting my paranoia keep me from attending what must have been a really spectacular event.

In truth, however, my "paranoia" wasn't that unwarranted. Shortly before receiving the invitation, we had been getting strange phone calls from people who wouldn't identify themselves, always wanting to know where Jess was, or if he had left for a certain lecture or commitment. Many times, the caller would leave a number for Jess to call, yet when Jess tried to call the person back, he would get a recording stating that the number was no longer working. And from the late 1980s to the early '90s, we would get calls in which no one would be on the other end of the line. For a while, it seemed this happened every time we had company—*but only when the subject of Roswell was brought up*. In fact, it was my mom who first brought to my attention the fact that the phone would mysteriously ring whenever the conversation turned to Roswell. We honestly began to wonder if our home was bugged, though we never found any evidence of this.

As a result of these strange calls, we became very secretive about Jess's meetings and travel itineraries. But still, the calls would come. Somewhere out there, someone was watching. The calls had ended in the early 1990s, but they still had us a bit shaken.

As Jess also related earlier, he received another puzzling phone call shortly before he left for Washington. This was from a person who wanted to meet with him at a location in the U.S. Capitol Building, claiming it was urgent. At this meeting, he asked Jess if we had ever been threatened. Jess told him about the strange, but not exactly threatening, telephone calls, whereupon the man gave him a number to call if we ever felt threatened. It was all very cloak-and-dagger, and had both Jess and I pretty concerned.

In 1994, we were off to California, to the premiere party for the TV movie *Roswell*, written and produced by Paul Davids, directed by Jeremy Kagan, and starring Kyle MacLachlan, Martin Sheen, and Dwight Yoakum. Kyle MacLachlan played the part of Jess's dad. The script was based on the book *UFO Crash At Roswell* by Kevin D. Randle and Donald R. Schmitt; some credit this movie—which was nominated for a Golden Globe Award—with truly bringing the Roswell Incident into the mainstream. The trip to Hollywood was quite an adventure for our family. Staying in the penthouse suite of the Universal Hilton and riding in limos, it was "country goes to the city!" Our girls were in heaven. In fact, I think this almost made up for the fear, uneasiness, and even embarrassment our kids sometimes felt in regard to the Roswell phenomenon. One of them actually had a very small part in the movie—so small that if you blinked, you would miss her. Her sisters were livid, as they figured that because the story was about her grandfather and father, she could have had more than fifteen *seconds* of fame.

In 1996, we were off to Paris for an appearance on a French television show. It was, naturally, done in French, so I could only understand Jess's part, and couldn't for the life of me tell you what the other stories were. Partway through Jess's interview, his face changed, and the MC wore a puzzled expression. Apparently, Jess's earphone had been inadvertently disconnected, and he could not hear the interpreter. As you would imagine, this rendered some of his answers completely bizarre. Our friend Kent Jeffrey and I had a hard time not laughing. Kent had been a big supporter of the effort to make the truth about Roswell public, as his father had apparently been in the Air Force, stationed at Roswell. At the time, Kent was trying to get a document known as the Roswell Initiative signed to force the government to release information on Roswell. For some reason, he later abandoned his efforts, and I guess we'll never know what changed his mind.

In July 1997, we chose to attend the 50th anniversary celebration in Roswell. Our youngest daughters had always been frightened about Roswell, so naturally we put off even telling them of our plans to attend, but the time finally had come, and we left for Roswell on one of the few driving trips we've taken. We usually fly, as we are time-limited and Jess is direction-impaired. But this time we thought it would be fun to take a road trip. We set off in the company of good friends, and toured Utah, the Grand Canyon, and Carlsbad Caverns along the way. When we arrived at Roswell, it was like entering another time, or, some would say, another dimension. The streets were crawling with Jeeps, driven by people dressed as aliens, some of which were actually quite convincing. In the shop windows were mannequins dressed as aliens. Everywhere you looked, there were people in costume, and vendors peddling anything even remotely related to UFOs, not to mention some of the most far-fringed products you'd ever imagine. It was like one big party, which—thankfully—served to elevate the girls' moods and make them completely forget that they had been afraid. For the next several days, our activities alternated between serious lectures and the carnival atmosphere on the street. I must admit, it was a wonderful time, and we got so caught up in the revelry that we almost forgot how deeply ingrained our lives had been with the original event.

In December of 1997, Jess came home from work and said, "I've got a conference to attend in Brazil. Anyone want to go?" We were all excited, until we were told that it was not safe to take the little girls. Guess who got to stay home *again*. Jess left for Brasilia in the beginning of December, and being the detail man that he is, had not left me his travel details. I had no idea where he was staying or when he'd be home. He later told me that he had met a Russian cosmonaut who had spent six months on the *Muir* space station, and had seen—you guessed it—a UFO.

After few days passed without hearing from Jess, I began to get worried. I checked the news to see if there had been any reports of planes crashing in the area. There were no crashes, so I told myself not to worry (I didn't listen), and I waited. After several more days went by without a word, my paranoia kicked in again. I was beginning to think he might have been abducted—not by aliens, but by Earthlings with sinister motives. The days turned into weeks. I did my Christmas shopping and attended Christmas parties alone. Everyone was asking me when he'd be home or if I'd heard from him, but there was still no news. Then, suddenly, one afternoon just before Christmas, he called and said that he was in California and would be home on the 11:00 plane. He acted as if he'd just been gone overnight. I was, to say the least, upset, and asked him—not too calmly—why he had not called. He said that it cost a hundred dollars to place a call from Brazil, and that if I wasn't home when he called, it would still cost the same. He said that, knowing me and that I'm seldom home, he thought he'd save money and call from the United States. I probably don't need to tell you that when he finally got home, and the initial relief at having him back safe and sound wore off, we had an in-depth discussion about the advisability of keeping in touch and the usefulness of the modern answering machine.

In 2006 we again returned to Roswell for the Fourth of July to test the waters and see if the time had come for Jess's book to be written. Jess had been encouraged throughout the years by so many people to write a book, and it felt as though the time had finally come for him to put pen to paper (so to speak). In 2004, Jess had been called back to active duty as a flight surgeon for the U.S. Army, and spent 13 months in Iraq. It was while he was stationed there that he began his effort in earnest. The atmosphere at Roswell in 2006, coupled with the strengthened resolve—and heightened sense of mortality—gained during his recent experience in Iraq, convinced him once and for all that he really needed to go full speed ahead with the book. Although Jess's concept of "full speed ahead" might not be completely consistent with some people's, his efforts throughout the last couple of years have been significant, and the result will, I hope, give the public a broader perspective on not just the events them- selves, but also the people involved.

From the U.S. Press Corps, to television documentaries, talk shows, radio shows and lectures in Brazil, Japan, Italy, France, and many U.S. cities, so many people had told their parts of the story, and Jess and his father had shared bits and pieces of theirs. But nowhere has the story been put into book form, by the one living person who possesses firsthand knowledge. I am truly glad that Jess has chosen this time to share his legacy with the world, for it is intimately tied to the Roswell story. Roswell has been a mixed blessing for our family, but as far I am concerned, Jess's love and admiration for his father—and his allegiance to truth in a culture that seems to thrive on deception—trump everything else in this story. I think his dad would be proud of his efforts. I know that I am.

~ Linda Marcel

CHAPTER 9
The Domino Effect

Many books have been written about the Roswell Incident, along with a seemingly endless stream of documentaries, movies, and editorial pieces, but none of them looked beyond the dates, times, and names surrounding that event, to examine what kind of effect Roswell has had upon the lives of those who actually lived it. And I can state with no hesitation whatsoever that the effect—at least upon me and those closest to me—has been significant. Linda's contributions in her chapter really brought that to light for me, and showed me that if readers are to have a clear picture of what Roswell meant and means, they need to be given an opportunity to read the story, as seen by those who actually lived it.

The best place to start any story is, of course, at the beginning, and the beginning of this story goes beyond the crash 60 years ago. It begins with the person at the center—my father, Jesse Marcel, Sr. He was so much more than just a footnote in history or an opinion to be accepted or refuted. And although I have already gone into his life story in a previous chapter, I believe that, in order to give you a clearer idea of how Roswell affected my life and my children's lives, it is worthwhile to dig a little deeper into my father's life, as well as his personality as it evolved throughout the years. That said, let's go back again for a moment.

Jesse Marcel, Sr., was an officer, a husband, a father, and a generous friend—a regular guy who got caught up in events bigger than himself, and handled those events and their repercussions pretty much as anyone who knew him would have expected. And to those who have painted a picture of him as anything else, well, they obviously didn't know him. And that is their loss.

As a kid, I can remember my dad being a pretty easygoing guy, albeit with strong opinions and deep passions. There was no doubt that he was a military man through and through, but that didn't mean he tried to run his home like a boot camp. Unlike the stereotypical career military man, he was perfectly willing to let others have their say without condemning them. And, as I've learned to appreciate since I became an adult, he was adept at being firm with the unbounded and unbridled energy of children, yet not so rigid as to stifle that energy. Was he perfect? Of course not. But, as I came to understand as I matured, the things that frustrate us the most are just the products of the same qualities we love the most about someone. I'll get into that a bit more later on.

As I noted early on in the book, from the time he was a kid, my father was fascinated with radio technology. Actually, *fascinated* might just be too mild a term. You may recall that he spent hard-earned money on parts to build his own radio, even knowing that he would get in trouble for doing so. It wasn't that he was rebellious. As a matter of fact, knowing him, I have wondered whether childhood rebellion had even been invented when he was growing up. No, he was a dutiful son—typical back then, but a rarity nowadays. The only thing that ran deeper than his respect for his parents was his hunger for knowledge. And he did his best to feed that hunger, not just as a kid, but all his life. That he was willing to go—albeit gently—against his mother's guidance in order to learn more about technology was but an early indicator of a pattern he would follow all his life, and that would ultimately be the source of his greatest sorrow, as well as his deepest joy.

By the time I came into the picture, Dad had really immersed himself in his life as an Army Air Corps officer. Some might say that in that life, he had the best of both worlds: the authority figures he could look up to and respect, as well as the opportunity to learn the details of how this new-fangled electronics technology worked. I can remember times when he would come home, excitedly telling my mother and I how he was learning so much about things that we couldn't even imagine, yet always reminding us that he couldn't say much about these things because it was his duty to keep the secrets to himself. Although he rarely talked much about *what* he was learning, I was always caught up in his palpable excitement, and I think it rubbed off on me somewhat. Because of his obvious passion, I developed a passion for learning myself.

He was also plainly fascinated with flying, and his many tales of flying with his buddies or the amazing capabilities of the airships of the day probably played a major role in my own fascination with airplanes. I came to understand that fathers can play a big part in forming their sons' interests—bigger, perhaps, than any of us fathers (or sons) would like to admit. And one area in which he had an enormous effect upon me was his love for the military.

To say that the military becomes one's parents, profession, and passion is actually not a big stretch at all. Even as a little kid, I knew that my father ate, drank, slept, and bled Army. He was very proud of what he did, and felt that he was fulfilling an important role in his country's well-being. I was proud of him for that, and he was truly the model from whom I would learn the definition of the word *honor*. It was only in later years that I began to understand how that code of honor could be diminished by the very people charged with keeping it alive.

When my father came home late that night in July of 1947, his excitement was obvious, and, frankly, contagious. Something big had happened, and we were all a part of it. Just how big, we had no idea. Yet in the months and years that followed, I saw my father change. Although there were still things that brought out a boyish excitement in him, I began seeing the edge of his passion blunted. He couldn't conceive of the reasons people he had trusted were acting differently toward him, or why people who were well aware of his capabilities and expertise had begun to question those capabilities and deny that expertise. And, as one would expect, the change in the institutions and people he had respected for so long began to take its toll on him.

It wasn't that he would come home and complain or speak badly about anybody, but it was obvious that he was troubled by what he was seeing. I occasionally heard him talking to my mother when they thought I was out of earshot, wondering what the heck was going on, and why people were so insistent upon saying things they knew were not the truth. In those days, it was common practice for a man to come home from a day at the office and sit down to a cocktail or two; it was more a ritual than anything else, I think—a silent declaration that the workday had ended, flowing naturally into the time for family, friends, and recreation. As time went on, I began to notice that the ritual cocktail or two became three, and then four, all before dinner. My parents' frequent bridge and bingo nights at the Officers' Club were all enhanced by copious amounts of liquid refreshment. The tension weighed on my mother as well, and she began drinking more heavily too.

I guess it would not be stretching things to say that my parents became alcoholics, though the word was never used in our home. The pressure they felt was clear, even to a child, and it got to the point that just about the only times I saw them acting as a loving, happy couple was after they had downed a few drinks. Eventually, even the reprieve they got from drinking began to diminish, and after my father finally left the military, alcohol seemed only to enhance their unhappiness, rather than mask it. As a child, I certainly didn't understand what had created the cloud that seemed to hang over them. All I knew was that my mother and father were no longer the happy couple I remembered.

In later years, that cloud seemed to grow even more impenetrable. My dad seemed to see people in a more negative light than he had previously. He would sometimes catch himself being overly critical of people he had revered in the past, and then the father I knew would reemerge for a time, reminding himself out loud that he wasn't being fair to them, even when his anger was probably more fair than his forgiveness. Eventually, even his actions toward my mother began to come under that cynical cloud. They didn't argue or fight, but it was obvious that there was a wall building between them, and their drinking—especially my mother's—became heavier and heavier as the years passed. Sadly, for the last 15 or 20 years of my mother's life, she suffered from a form of dementia common to people who drank heavily for many years.

Sometimes I wondered whether I might be to blame for some of their growing distance from each other, and I tried harder to be a good son to compensate. I even wondered whether my dad might have grown angry with me for some reason, because he didn't seem to enjoy doing things with me as much. For many years, I figured that the distance between us was supposed to be there; a product of my growing up. It took many years to figure out, but I eventually realized that it wasn't I who was coming between my parents, and that the distance that seemed to be growing between my dad and me had nothing to do with growing up, or with anything I had done. Rather, it was my father's reaction to his deep and growing disillusionment with his beloved military, the sense that he had devoted so much of his life to something, only to be spit out when he became "inconvenient." He was also affected by the growing clamor of those who felt the need to belittle everything for which he stood and for which he had worked so hard throughout his adult life.

To his dying day, he would never come out and actually condemn the military, and I have to believe that even his long-enduring sense of loyalty only added to his bitterness. The closest he ever came to that condemnation was when I was about 14 years old, just about the time the Korean War was beginning. He came home one night and proclaimed, "I'm getting out of this! I'm tired of taking orders!" That was one of the few times I ever got angry at my father, and I told him—with all the moral authority of a 14-year-old—that he couldn't quit during a war. He just looked at me for a second, shook his head, and went into the other room. Without his speaking another word, that look told me that there were things I just didn't understand, and he hoped I never would. It was many years before I was able to completely comprehend the volumes he had spoken in that silent moment. I wish there was a way for me to let him know that I finally got it. It took my own service in another war—this one in the desert of Iraq, a mission in which I firmly believe—before I could truly understand the changes he went through.

I believe I can speak with some authority on what he was going through, because I have endured much of the same kind of feelings and experiences in my own life. The biggest difference is that I learned early on that upping the number of after-hours cocktails doesn't make things better, and that the one true remedy for disillusionment is found in the time spent with the people I love. My father taught me, even if unknowingly, to hold tightly to truth and to those people who valued me for what I *am*, rather than where I stood on any given issue. It is because of him that I am able to stand up and tell what I know—and have always known—to be true, realizing that there will always be someone who will try to discredit what I say, and, by extension, me.

Not surprisingly, the legacy of Roswell—the story as well as the doubts and the emotional strain that comes with those doubts—has carried on through three generations in my family. That it affected my parents and me should come as no surprise to anyone. That it has had such a profound effect upon my own children, however, caught even me by surprise.

Growing up in a home where the reality of alien visitation is accepted as fact can be very frightening to a child. It wasn't that we sat around the dinner table every night talking about creatures from outer space, but rather that Linda's and my attitude toward the whole idea was pretty blasé. As a matter of fact, the topic of UFOs rarely ever came up during family discussions. We weren't members of the tin-foil hat group, who sat around contemplating when the next visit would occur, and when we saw something on television or in the paper about people who claimed to have been abducted or to be in contact with alien visitors, we probably laughed at their stories as much as anyone else.

When we had friends over, however, and especially when we entertained people who were active in UFO research, the children would naturally overhear our conversations. Lacking the sense of security that usually comes with adulthood, the children's perception was that of a danger to themselves and us that we adults simply never considered. Perhaps it would have been better for them if I had insulated them from the subject when they were little, but given that most of the people we knew were aware that I was the guy who had actually handled pieces of a "flying saucer," keeping the children in the dark would have been awfully hard—if not impossible—to do. So, for better or for worse, the children found themselves pretty much in the middle of the whole UFO controversy, especially where the incident at Roswell was concerned.

Linda and I have talked with the children—who are all adults now—on numerous occasions about UFOs and what they had thought and felt about the subject while they were growing up. They were, at various times and depending upon the particular child, frightened, embarrassed, bored, or indifferent.

As far as their relationship with the man who started it all, I have to say that none of our kids was ever very close to my dad. He lived in Louisiana and we lived in Montana, and visits were rare. I spoke to my mom and dad every Sunday, but the kids rarely did. Even after my father passed away and my mom came to live with Linda and me, the kids never became very close to their grandmother. Nevertheless, Roswell was part of their lives.

Our daughter MacKenzie told us that she remembers always being frightened that the aliens would come someday and abduct her and her older sister, Marissa. She said that when we used to drive to our condo in Big Sky to ski, she worried that aliens would come and get us. She went on to explain that she was most afraid when we were driving at night through a canyon to get to the mountain, where she feared the aliens could swoop down and take us without anybody seeing what happened, and no one would ever know what had become of us all.

She also said she was scared when we went to California for the premier of the TV movie *Roswell*. At the premier, my step-daughter Ashlee, who was 19 or 20 at the time, was in heaven with all the attention she was getting. While attending the festivities, we stayed in the Universal Hilton penthouse, an environment that, to the kids, must have been as wondrous as the Emerald City of Oz. I remember chuckling at Linda at the time, because the windows of our suite were all glass, and due to Linda being terrified of heights, she made us keep all the curtains pulled. As one would imagine, trying to block such a magnificent view from children who were in awe of it was a significant challenge.

The premier party was incredibly exciting to the girls, who had their first opportunity to see so many celebrities up close and in person. Linda, however, didn't have a clue who these people were, because she never watched television, and paid no attention to the "who's who" of the movie world.

My daughter Denice has always been interested in science fiction, and wasn't afraid as was MacKenzie. Similar to many young girls, she had dreams of being a movie star. When Paul Davids gave her a brief part in *Roswell*, she was on cloud nine. (If you look quickly and pay close attention, she is the waitress in the officer's club when Glenn Dennis meets with the mystery nurse.)

The producers had a limo pick us up to take us to the premiere, and MacKenzie, who was around 10 years old at the time, thought that perhaps the aliens had sent it. All through the showing, MacKenzie kept her eyes tightly shut, and wouldn't watch the movie because it scared her so badly. We couldn't even watch an innocent movie like *ET* because she was so afraid. She lived in fear that the "gray people," as she called them, would get her.

Even as an adult, she admits that some of that fear remains. MacKenzie told us that when we went to Roswell for the 50th anniversary of the crash, when she was 12, she was still apprehensive, fearing that it was a likely time for the aliens to show up. Furthermore, she did not like being around everyone wearing alien costumes, probably because she figured that a real alien could easily hide among them until the opportunity presented itself to snatch us up. She even hated all the alien paraphernalia everywhere you looked.

I was never really sure what her older sister Marissa felt, as she never seemed to make a big deal of the whole alien thing, one way or the other. When she was in high school and college, people would frequently ask her if she was related to Jesse Marcel. In fact, on one occasion, she was having dinner at her roommate's parents' house when the adults started talking about Roswell. She said that she just sat quietly and listened to the conversation, until finally her roommate said that the little boy they were talking about was Marissa's dad. At that point, she said, everyone turned and stared at her, which was pretty uncomfortable. They apparently hadn't connected the Marcel name, but once the secret was out, they all got very excited, and deluged Rissa with all kinds of questions. I can only imagine how that must have felt to her.

Aimee and Ashlee were typical teenage girls, whose primary reaction to their stepfather's fame, such as it was, could be summed up in one word: *embarrassment*. Similar to all teenagers, they wanted to stand out with their peers, but not for something their stepfather had done. I'm sure that they were the brunt of some teasing by the other kids—nothing really serious or malicious, but cruel in the way that kids of all ages tend to be. As a result, they acted as though the whole UFO/ Roswell scenario simply didn't exist, and if one of their friends mentioned seeing me on television, they would change the subject as quickly as possible.

I'm certain that the family's immersion in the UFO controversy had its effect on how we looked at other things as well. For example, I can remember that when we lived in our 1880s mansion in Helena, Rissa and Linda told me that they were always seeing an unexplainable green light floating around inside the place. Many strange things happened in that house, but we always thought it was the ghost of Mrs. Tatum, the lady who had first lived there. But maybe MacKenzie was closer to knowing the real source after all. We'll probably never know, but it was good for more than one interesting conversation at family dinners!

One day, sometime in the middle '70s, I was driving home with my sons Jay and John, and we all saw a strange object a little ways south of where we were, flying from the east to the west against a fairly strong prevailing wind. We immediately jumped out and stood in the yard to get a better look. Even though it obviously had to be under its own power to fly against the wind, it made virtually no sound. The total time it was visible was less than half a minute, and we were all completely awed by what we had seen. After it had passed out of sight, the three of us went into the house and independently drew pictures of what we had just seen. When we compared our drawings, each one looked virtually identical to the others: Each drawing was of a classic disc-shaped UFO (though John's drawing was really kind of a teardrop-shaped blob). Considering that he was only six or seven years old at the time, I thought he did a pretty good job of capturing the image. Needless to say, we were all excited by the experience. I had actually forgotten about the event until they reminded me about it, and I had been saying for years that I had never seen one of those things. Memory is a strange thing. Something that you think never existed comes back in a flash. Maybe some part of me was trying to suppress it for the last 30 years or so, though I'm certain that some people would proclaim that I had been abducted, and that the "little green men" had erased my memory. I figure, if that's what they find most entertaining...

Jay and John were always interested in science fiction, and loved to look through our telescope at the moon and stars. In fact, all the kids enjoyed the times we spent on cloudless nights, searching the heavens. The boys and I liked flying the radio-controlled planes and helicopters we built, and because we have usually lived in areas without power poles, we had plenty of opportunities to fly them in the fields. They loved to make bottle rockets and send them aloft in the foothills around our house, to the never-ending amazement of their friends. They also enjoyed creating electrical circuits, helping me build Tesla coils, and "inventing" all kinds of electrical circuits, some of which actually did something useful (or at least entertaining). I knew they were having a good time, and tried to keep a fairly close eye on what they were creating (especially because Linda pretty much lived in fear that they would blow up the house or set it on fire—which, thankfully, they never did, though they sometimes came closer than I chose to tell her).

Even as interested as the boys were in all things scientific, they tended to feel uncomfortable with the UFO aspect of our lives as they were growing up. As we all know, young boys will use anything they can find to get a leg up on the other boys in their crowd, and Jay and John ended up being the target of a lot of teasing, simply because there was something about them that differentiated them from their friends—namely, that their dad had seen and handled a UFO. Tease a kid enough, especially about his parents, and he will either start to avoid you or get right in your face, sometimes with a fist. I don't think the boys got into that many fights over my UFO connection, and probably wouldn't have told me if they did. They were, for the most part, well-behaved and good natured, but as do all young boys, they lived by a code that demanded that they keep some things secret from Mom and Dad. Besides, I know all too well how even the telling of an unhappy event can make it seem even more real and more important, and feeling embarrassed about your dad is not something to which a kid wants to give any more substance.

Just as any parent, I've regretted the discomfort, the fear, and the embarrassment that my father's and my experiences have caused for my family. Even now, the specter of Roswell is creating rifts in our family, causing me no end of despair. I've been asked many times whether I would prefer that the Roswell Incident never have happened at all, and I must admit that there have been times when I felt that life would have been a lot easier, and my family's and my path much smoother, had we never even heard of Roswell.

But then again, I recall the wonder in my father's eyes, and the sense of awe that must have shown in mine, and I realize that, despite the challenges it brought to my parents, my wife, my children, and myself, the events of that July evening 60 years ago represent something infinitely more important than the inconveniences we might have endured as a result. That night offered humanity a rare opportunity to look beyond its petty squabbles, and even beyond the boundaries of this tiny planet on which we live. It gave us a glimpse of a greater universe, and the chance to make the most of our place in it. And to my way of thinking, the "insurmountable" hassles we have faced as a result are a pretty cheap price to pay. My hope is that we can one day be allowed to know the truth, and perhaps to even look back on our resistance to that truth with the same benign judgment we apply to the things we did as little children. For, in the grand universal scheme of things, perhaps little children are what we are after all.

CHAPTER 10
Life in the Cosmos:
Beyond Roswell

As I pointed out early in this book, I am not attempting to write the be-all and end-all work on the topic of extraterrestrial life, the technology involved in space travel, or even the final analysis of what happened near Roswell back in 1947. Those topics would require many tomes of far greater volume and depth than this one.

Like my father before me, I have been filled with an insatiable scientific curiosity all my life, particularly on subjects arising from my early experiences. I have done extensive research in the areas of ufology, quantum physics, alien visitations and abductions, humans' attempts to communicate with other worlds, and even the incredibly dynamic physical makeup of our own planet. (To give you an idea of the depth of my obsession with the latter, I once even built my own seismograph, with which I was able to measure earthquakes all over the world.) I won't bore you with *all* of the fascinating facts and theories I have encountered, but I do want to share a few tidbits of the work that has been and is being done to discover the answers to the question, "Are we alone?"

First, to give you a perspective of how vast the distances in the universe are, if the sun were the size of a period on this page, the Earth would be an invisible speck an inch away, and the nearest star would be 3/4 of a mile off. A passenger plane would take 5 million years to make the voyage to the nearest star, and it would take a billion years to walk it. These facts open the door to all kinds of problems with interstellar travel, which we will need major scientific breakthroughs to overcome. We know that some civilizations have made this leap, because they are visiting us from their parent systems. If they can do it, then we can—and *will*, given time. Considering the insatiable human curiosity and our need to advance, I have no doubt that we will accomplish space travel and join other spacefaring civilizations soon enough.

Breakthroughs Necessary for Space Travel

A significant part of some people's unwillingness to accept the existence of visitors from another world lies in the extraordinary distance between Earth and its closest potential neighbor. Although our modes of travel here on Earth—as well as our forays into our solar system—have progressed dramatically in our lifetime, we still rely upon technologies that are dependent upon a crude action-reaction process, and we comprehend speed in miles per hour, or, at best, feet per second. Travel to planets in other solar systems at speeds of which we are presently capable would take more years than have passed throughout all of humankind's recorded history. And even if we were to attempt a trip lasting many millennia, the amount of fuel we would have to carry would weigh more than we could even get off the ground, to say nothing of getting it high enough to escape Earth's gravitational pull. To give an example of how daunting the challenge would be, the amount of rocket fuel it would take to propel a large bus to the nearest star in 900 years would outweigh the universe! And for those of you who immediately ask, "Why not use a nuclear fission–powered rocket?" it has been calculated that it would take a billion super-tankers full of nuclear fuel to get the bus to the nearest star in only 900 years. Of course, using a fusion-powered rocket would save an immense amount of weight, but such a rocket would still require a thousand supertankers filled with fuel. For those of you who are science fiction aficionados familiar with antimatter propulsion, it has been calculated that it would take merely 10 railway tanker cars filled with antimatter to make the trip, but we are still talking about a 900-year, one-way journey. Given these present limitations, it is not surprising that some people remain skeptical of the possibility that others have actually accomplished things that we have difficulty even imagining.

However, NASA has some out-of-the-box ideas about breaking the theoretical light-speed limit of special relativity, which states that any object with mass cannot exceed or even approach the speed of light. Although massive objects have to obey this rule, space itself is not limited to the speed of light, and can expand at any arbitrary pace, with no limit. The Alcubierre drive, named after its creator, Mexican physicist Miguel Alcubierre, who proposed the idea in a 1994 issue of the *Journal of Classical and Quantum Gravity*, demonstrates this possibility. In the Alcubierre drive, the space ahead of a spacecraft is compressed, while the space behind it is expanded. As a result, the space in which the craft is contained is pulled from ahead *and* pushed from behind. To an outside observer, the person in the craft would be traveling faster than light, but in the passenger's capsule of space, he or she would feel no acceleration forces. For all practical purposes, he or she would be sitting still, while the immediate environment would be traveling at a speed that is—at least in theory—limitless. Because the craft embedded in this capsule of space is not subject to acceleration forces, its occupants would not be violently thrashed about during high-speed maneuvering. The catch is, contracting space in the front would take a huge amount of positive energy, and expanding space in the back would require an equal amount of negative energy. The technology for generating such immense levels of energy—not to mention proving even the existence of the phenomenon—does not currently exist on Earth, but might be possible within the realm of quantum physics, which civilizations on other worlds may well have already harnessed.

The following is a diagram of the distortion of space-time produced by the Alcubierre space drive.

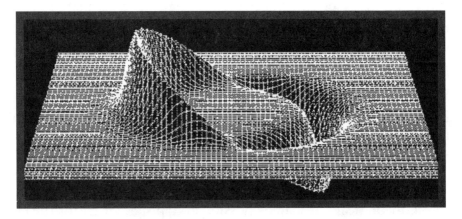

Space-time warped by the Alcubierre drive.

One analogy of this capsule of space carrying its passenger faster than the surrounding space-time continuum is the moving sidewalk in an airline terminal. Visualize the moving sidewalk as the capsule with its passenger, and the fixed floor as the surrounding space-time. The moving sidewalk adds its forward speed to the passenger walking on it, so, to the passenger, he or she is walking at a normal speed, but still passes people walking on the fixed floor.

Another technology currently being researched by NASA is the Variable Specific Impulse Magnetoplasma Rocket (VASIMR). VASIMR is a plasma-based propulsion system that uses an electric power source to ionize fuel, converting it to plasma. Electric fields heat and accelerate the plasma, while the magnetic fields focus the stream of plasma as it is ejected from the engine. This creates thrust for the spacecraft, which can be controlled much like the rocket-propelled engines we currently use. The VASIMR can be fueled by hydrogen, which is the most plentiful element in the universe, thus eliminating the need to carry the tremendous amount of fuel required for a prolonged trip. The required electric power could be provided by a nuclear generator, or by photovoltaic (solar) panels for trips that are relatively close to the sun. Although VASIMR is still being researched, and is years away from practical application, it has already shown enough promise during tests on Earth for scientists to be hopeful. However, the VASIMR engine would still only be capable of attaining speeds much slower than the speed of light, rendering it useful only for travel within our own solar system.

NASA is also investigating a type of warp drive that may be closer than we might think. Rather than carrying the fuel necessary for space travel, theoretically, it may be possible to tap space itself for the energy source. This so-called *zero-point energy field* theoretically contains energy greater than nuclear density. The proof of principle has been established tapping this energy (in other words, the idea has been proven mathematically valid), so all it takes now is the engineering (this would be a step beyond the matter-antimatter engines of the starship *Enterprise*). As we know from the theory of special relativity, no massive particle can travel faster than the speed of light, no matter how much energy you have. As previously discussed, space itself is not constrained by this law. But empty space is not empty. It consists of a field called the *false vacuum*, which is filled with energetic particles that pop in and out of a fleeting existence. There is experimental evidence that these particles exist along with an incredible amount of energy called the *zero point energy*. With that said, there is proof of principle that there is a fundamental relationship between time, gravity, and inertia. If you can alter one, you can alter the other, and experiments indicate that indeed time, gravity, and inertia *can* be altered. That would provide another way for faster-than-light travel to be, at least theoretically, possible. At this time we don't have the engineering to put it into practice, but again, the proof of principle is at hand.

If we are already thinking along these lines, it does not take much of a leap of faith that others who are farther along technologically have developed the engineering, put it into practice, and made space travel a reality. (I get a kick out of reading these all-knowing statements from less imaginative scientists that interstellar travel is impossible because *we* can't do it. The conclusion is that because interstellar travel is impossible, none of these UFO sightings can be interstellar spacecraft.)

Yet another technology that has not been tested, but shows some promise, is Robert W. Bussard's "Ramjet." Very simply, the Bussard engine is composed of a large sail to collect hydrogen atoms, which it then feeds to a nuclear reactor. The resulting nuclear explosions would provide incredible levels of thrust, allowing the vehicle to gradually accelerate to near-light speeds. The craft would putt-putt across space, with each successive putt increasing its speed exponentially. There are, however, drawbacks to this technology: Chief among obstacles to even testing the design is the Outer Space Treaty, which entered into force on October 10, 1967. This treaty, onto which virtually all industrialized countries signed, prohibits the detonation of potentially harmful nuclear explosions in space. Because the Bussard engine in operation is literally a constant chain of nuclear explosions, we are severely limited in our ability to even test it, much less apply the technology to our space travel aspirations.

We are on the doorstep of becoming a spacefaring civilization. We have made giant strides in exploring our backyard with planetary probes of our own. We are on the verge of finding life on other planets, such as Mars, and have sent sophisticated probes that roam its surface, studying its interesting geology and weather patterns. Some of our probes are destined to travel out of our system and actually head into interstellar space, such as *Pioneer 10*, which was launched in

March of 1972. The last signal received from it was January 22, 2003; it is thought that its radio-isotope thermal generator finally went dead, shutting its transmitter off. It is headed in the general direction of Aldebaran, in the constellation Taurus, some 82 light-years away, and it should get there in about 2 million years. It bears a gold plaque that gives any intelligent civilization information about us, even though we may be long gone by the time they find it. This plaque was designed by Frank Drake and Carl Sagan.

Pioneer 10 heading out into interstellar space.

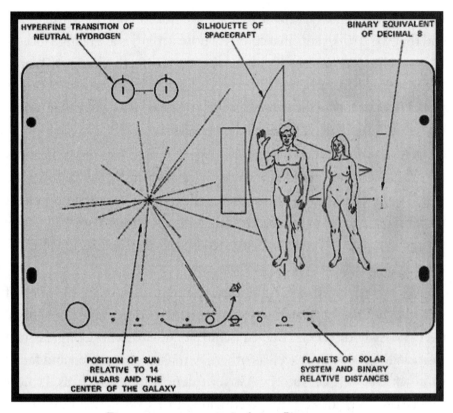

The message carried on *Pioneer 10.*

Secrecy

Why does our government (and other world governments) not tell the truth about UFOs? Why all the secrecy? I think that the people of Earth deserve to know the true nature of what is really out there. I have pondered this question for years, as have many others—most of whom are more knowledgeable than I in these matters. To answer the *why* of UFO secrecy, I can only guess: Is it because the powers that be feel they have to protect us from ourselves? In other words, can we really stand to know the ultimate truth of the nature of some UFOs, that they represent an advanced civilization studying us? It would be rather unnerving to discover that we are not in control of our skies, and that we are like ants in a colony whose activities are being studied. Our feelings of superiority were already stripped when our planet was displaced from being the center of the solar system to a minor planet orbiting an ordinary star in the outskirts of a galaxy that is only one of innumerable galaxies in the universe.

NASA has conducted a survey of what would happen if the news of our descent into mediocrity was made known by the fact that we were being visited by an advanced civilization. The surprising result is that most people would accept this without undue alarm. The only people who would really be disturbed by this are the religious fundamentalists who feel God created *only* us.

My thoughts on the rigid secrecy range through a number of reasons. It may be that most government people have no control over the issue of UFOs. Steven Schiff, a New Mexico Congressman from 1989 to 1998, as well as other lawmakers, have tried and failed to crack the veil of secrecy. Government studies such as Project Bluebook and Project Grudge concluded that there was nothing of value in pursuing the investigation of reported UFO sightings, and Dr. J. Allen Hyneck, who ran the Bluebook inquiry, was a total debunker, who gave explanations such as "swamp gas" when he was attached to Bluebook. Once he was no longer a member of the team, however, he started to change his opinion of the UFO phenomena, and was open to the reality that at least some of these sightings may represent exotic phenomena such as extraterrestrial spacecraft.

One would think that since the Freedom of Information Act (FOIA) was passed, information on UFO activity would be much more accessible. Yeah, right! As UFO researchers such as Stanton Friedman soon found out, you may get reams of pages after a suitably long wait, but these pages are basically useless, because they are mostly blacked out. This of course means that there are some details in these UFO sightings about which someone doesn't want the general public to know. This purposeful withholding of information is prime evidence that there is something going on that must be kept from the public domain. If the government says these reports are either hoaxes or just confused people, then why is it necessary to withhold information? That leaves two possibilities: Either these really are extraterrestrial craft that we must be protected from knowing about, or they are highly classified military aircraft. I don't believe all the sightings could be of highly classified military aircraft; there is no doubt in my mind that some of these sightings are from exotic craft, such as those from another civilization.

Apparently the powers that be feel that we common folk don't need to know about it. It is disturbing to think that the reason why the full story of UFOs isn't disclosed is that the truth is something we truly don't want to know, and that we are being kept in blissful ignorance for a good reason. President Reagan made a statement at an address at the United Nations in which he suggested that the whole world would suddenly become united should there be a threat from without, even going so far as to wonder whether an alien force was already among us. Did President Reagan know of a possible extraterrestrial threat, his statement a gentle reminder and tacit admission that we are not alone? One wonders what will happen when overt, undeniable contact occurs. But, as I implied earlier, the fact that we are still here suggests that any alien species observing us is of a benign character.

The Odds on Life

You have to ask why there is life in this universe. Was it created by a Creator, or is it just a result of a series of unlikely events? One could ask, is there just one universe? Or are there a multitude of universes, the so-called multiverse? Either way, just by the odds, I believe there have to be many other civilizations out there. It has been said that if we are the only life, then there is a lot of wasted space. My personal feeling is that we and the universe were created by a Creator. The universe had to be incredibly fine-tuned for life to exist, and I for one don't believe that all that extra space is wasted. Putting the UFO phenomena aside, at this moment, planet Earth is the only site where life is recognized to exist by traditional science. Sadly, until traditional science accepts the reality that events such as Roswell were indeed extraterrestrial craft, humanity will have to accept the presence of intelligent life elsewhere on faith. I have to confess that, had I not seen the debris from that craft on our kitchen floor, I would look at the UFO phenomena with a bit of skepticism. Again, leaving UFO events aside, there are compelling arguments to suggest that we are not alone. Most astrophysicists would agree that there is a high probability of not only life, but *intelligent* life existing elsewhere, just based on the laws of physics and chance. There are 10^{22} stars in the visible universe, a number that equates to the number of sand grains on Earth. No matter how unlikely the possibility of life on any given star, there are so many chances for life to exist on a multitude of planets. This means that there is nothing special about this planet, its location in the galaxy, or even our galaxy's place in the universe.

Our own galaxy of 200 to 400 billion stars (which would equate to the number of salt grains it would take to fill an Olympic-sized swimming pool) has innumerable solar systems. The Hubble Space Telescope (HST) has determined that planetary systems that at one time were considered to be very rare are now known to be commonplace. The HST has visualized protoplanetary discs around stars where planetary systems are still in their embryonic or cocoon stage. Maybe just a small fraction of these will go on to develop Earth-like planets with life, but the sheer numbers dictate that there must be many, many such planets that are the abodes of intelligent, spacefaring civilizations. As it turns out, the stars that have the same spectral features as our sun are the ones most likely to have an accompanying retinue of planets.

So far we have found at least 130 extra-solar planets through a variety of means. No true Earth-like planet has yet been found, but our instruments are not quite at the sensitivity to discover Earth look-alikes. Once we find another Earth-like planet, studies can be made of its atmosphere to determine if its gasses contain water vapor, oxygen, and nitrogen. If these are found, life is almost a certainty, especially if there is a trace of methane present. Methane is a biological marker, and its presence would be difficult to explain in the absence of life. Methane has been detected in the Martian atmosphere, which is a very strong clue that life similar to ours is present. Because methane is a gas that degrades, it would be completely gone in 300 years, unless it is continually replaced by volcanic activity, cometary collisions, or biologic activity. Because there is no known volcanic activity or recent cometary collisions on Mars, current biologic activity would almost certainly have to be present.

In 1984, a meteorite named ALH 84001 was found in the Allan Hills region of Antarctica that apparently came to Earth about 13,000 years ago. After study, it was determined that it indeed did come from Mars, and was probably knocked off the surface by a meteorite impact. Gasses contained in the meteorite were consistent with the atmospheric gasses known to be on Mars. Further study revealed some remarkable findings: There were abundant amounts of polycyclic aromatic hydrocarbons (PAHs) that can be produced by organic activity. It is known that some PAHs found in meteorites can be from inorganic activity, but the type found in the Martian meteorite was consistent with the type produced by biology. In conjunction with the PAHs there were also unusual minerals found. They were carbonate globules about 50 microns across, with cores containing manganese, rings of iron carbonate and sulfides, along with magnetite and pyrorhite. These all bear strong resemblances to mineral alterations identical to those produced by primitive Earth bacteria. The pattern found in the magnetite was identical to the pattern produced by Earth bacteria, so finding all of this in such a small area makes a nonbiological origin unlikely. The most startling of all findings was made by a high-resolution electron microscope. It found what appear to be almost certainly fossilized bacteria. These are very small, and would be classified as *nanobes*. Taking all of these findings together makes a biological origin most likely. In other words, "if it looks like a skunk and smells like a skunk, then it is probably a skunk." Taking the Occam's razor concept that if you have a variety of solutions to a problem, the simplest explanation is the most likely one, that would be biology.

The Mars meteorite thought to contain fossilized bacteria.

Our sun is a third-generation star, which means that two previous generations of stars went through their life cycles, with us being the beneficiary of their ashes. Some 13.7 billion years ago our universe was born in the "big bang," which produced clouds primarily made of hydrogen and helium with a trace of other elements such as deuterium. These clouds of deuterium and helium provided fuel for the first-generation stars, which went through their life cycles to produce heavier elements in a supernova explosion. It took one more generation of stars to produce the elements of which our solar system is made. If it happened here, it most assuredly happened elsewhere, and perhaps much sooner, so those civilizations would be older and wiser. Even a span of a few thousand years would put them vastly ahead with their technology.

I was fortunate enough recently to hear Dr. Edgar Mitchell of *Apollo 14*, the sixth man to walk on the moon, give a talk for the Paradigm Research Group, an organization dedicated to the disclosure of UFO secrets from various governmental agencies. In that talk, he spoke of his forebears settling in Texas after getting there in a covered wagon. A hundred years later, Ed was walking on the face of the moon. If we can do that in a hundred years, what would a thousand years do for us? Unfortunately, with our advances in science and space technology, we have also had advances in weapons technology. We can now thoroughly annihilate ourselves, and have come breathtakingly close to doing so in the last several decades. Perhaps some promising civilizations have done exactly that, and have extinguished themselves. I speculate that some of our space cousins have taken an increased interest in us because of our self-destructive tendencies, and may be taking bets to see if we survive to join the intergalactic club of space-faring civilizations. If we continue on our current rate of technological advancement for the next several hundred years, we will be well on our way to the stars.

For many years, the Roman Catholic Church taught that the Earth was the center of everything, and this view was supported by Ptolemy based on the then-known orbits of the planets. It was Copernicus who determined that the planets orbited the sun, and not the other way around. With each discovery we were further displaced down the rungs of a very long ladder. It is now known that even our solar system is in the outskirts of a common galaxy, and our galaxy's place is not unique in a universe of a hundred billion galaxies. Life on this planet is found in just about every nook and cranny, from the deepest ocean trenches to the boiling pools of Yellowstone; it seems that the only requirements for life as we know it are water and a source of energy.

In 1584, a Dominican priest and philosopher named Giordano Bruno wrote, "There are countless suns and countless Earths all rotating around their suns in exactly the same way as the seven planets of our system. We see only the suns because they are the largest bodies and are luminous, but their planets remain invisible to us because they are smaller and non-luminous. The countless worlds in our universe are no worse and no less inhabited than our Earth." In 1600, he was burned at the stake for his words. Although we no longer punish people in such a way for belief in extraterrestrial civilizations, there are still some who would attempt to destroy the reputations of those who are believers, with one popular televangelist actually advocating that they be stoned to death, according to the Old Testament custom for punishing heretics. Fortunately, the majority of our population is enlightened enough not to consider such a barbaric reaction.

Contact

The SETI (Search for Extraterrestrial Intelligence) program is seeking an artificial radio signal from afar, but so far no definite signals have been received. There have been false alarms, such as from pulsar stars, satellites, or aircraft, but alas, no genuine signals. There has been one possible signal that cannot be proven to be natural, and it is being studied more closely. The signal is designated SHGb02+14a, and has been picked up several times. It is thought to originate several thousand light-years away, and does not appear to be produced by any known natural means. It has a frequency of 1420 MHz, which is the most likely frequency to be selected by an extraterrestrial civilization to broadcast a radio alert, because it is in a relatively quiet zone, and free of natural interference. If it does prove to be artificial, it would have been broadcast several thousand years ago, and there is no telling what the originators of that signal are doing now.

The giant radio telescopes of the Arecibo Observatory, capable of sending messages to the stars.

Some years ago, the radio telescope at Arecibo, Puerto Rico, sent out a signal that, if deciphered, would tell a little about us as human beings and where we live in the galaxy. It was sent out to a globular cluster some 80,000 light-years away. In the signal, the first set of symbols (white) represents the numbers 1 to 10, reading from right to left. The cluster in the center (purple) codes the atomic numbers for certain elements. The green-colored patterns represent formulas for sugars and bases in nucleotides of DNA. The white vertical bar specifies the number of nucleotides in DNA. The double helix of DNA is represented by the blue curving lines that go from the sugars/base formulas to the human being. The next symbol to the left of the human figure represents the human population on Earth, and the ones to the right side of the human figure represent the height of a human being. The yellow symbols represent our solar system, with the Earth displaced upward to the human figure. The purple symbols represent the Arecibo Telescope, and the white and blue symbols on the bottom represent its diameter.

Some people are worried about these attempts at contacting an extraterrestrial civilization, because we have no way of knowing how they would perceive and react to knowledge of our existence. In fact, though, it is a bit late to hide our presence: Our radio and television signals have been broadcasting our presence for 80 years. Television signals dating back to the Berlin Olympics in 1936 are now passing stars up to 70 light-years away. (The Carl Sagan book *Contact* was based on the scenario that these signals were picked up and responded to, but because of the tremendous distance of 26 light-years, we did not receive their response until 52 years later.) Like it or not, we have made our presence known to ETs that may be in star systems up to 80 light-years away.

We can hope that the extraterrestrials visiting us are more like E.T. than the ones depicted in *Independence Day*. But the truth is, both types are probably out there, and we are lucky that the ones in our skies appear to be more like E.T., the botanist. We know full well what happens when an advanced civilization comes into contact with one that is less advanced; we have plenty of examples here on Earth: What happens first is conflict, then subjugation, and finally assimilation. So far, none of this seems to be happening with our experiences. The more likely scenario is that we are a scientific curiosity to be studied rather than interacted with.

We know that there are spacefaring civilizations out there, and, moreover, that they have shown an interest in us with their investigatory probes. If you believe in the abduction phenomena, then you have to consider that these beings have taken a personal interest in us. Reputable investigators such as Budd Hopkins are conducting strong research that is difficult to refute, although significant effort has been expended by some skeptics to do so. Knowing Budd as I do, and being aware of the methods he uses in his research, I have to believe that, on rare occasions, alien abductions must occur. I think they are studying us just as we would study other life forms here on Earth. I believe that these beings have a keen scientific interest in our physical and scientific development, and that they don't represent a danger to us, and we don't have anything they want—if we did, we would not be here.

A significant number of rather interesting discoveries in places all over the world suggest that Earth has been of interest to extraterrestrial visitors for thousands of years. There are ancient cave paintings of humanoid creatures clad in what appear to be protective suits such as space suits, complete with helmets. Primitive drawings have been discovered of inhuman creatures with round heads and large eyes. In some Egyptian tombs, pictures have been found of what appear to be aircraft. In the Nasca Plains south of Lima, Peru, alongside line drawings of animals are seeming depictions of airfields and runways. These drawings are imperceptible from the ground, and so were not discovered until the 20th century, when people began flying over the area. England boasts similar ancient drawings that can only be seen in complete context from the air. The existence of such artifacts raises the question: Why would the ancients spend the time and effort to make line drawings that can only be appreciated from a vantage point that they are unable to reach?

More recently, during the Renaissance period, a famous painting was created of the Madonna and Child, with a saucer-shaped craft shown hovering in the nearby sky; a man and a dog are looking skyward at the object. Going back a bit further, there are even biblical accounts of what could well be UFO encounters, such as Ezekiel's "wheel"— he witnessed and described typical UFO apparitions. The ancients described them as objects familiar to them, such as chariots, shields, and flaming wheels. Similarly, today we describe such sightings in relation to objects that are familiar to us, such as cigar shapes, saucer shapes, flying triangles, and the like.

In 1897, there was an intriguing—yet reasonably contested— account of a sighting throughout the Midwest, where people reported seeing what they described as "airships" flying through the air. This was years before the Wright Brothers first flew at Kitty Hawk, and although there were hot air balloons at that time, it was obvious that what people were seeing were *not* balloons. In April of that year, a flying object crashed into a windmill on a ranch outside of Aurora, Texas. When the site was investigated, considerable damage was seen to have been done to the windmill, and the remains of the object were lying about the area. People reported seeing strange writing on the pieces of debris, but the strangest remains were that of the apparent pilot. The description given by a number of people at the time was of a nonhuman being. This being was given a Christian burial in the town cemetery, and the remains of the craft were dumped down a well. That well has now been bricked over, and investigators have long been denied permission to excavate it. Likewise, permission could not be obtained to excavate the grave of the being, and the grave marker disappeared long ago. One artifact has been recovered from the site, which was quite weathered, indicating it had been there for years. Analysis showed that it was an alloy of aluminum and iron that would be difficult to manufacture, and for which there is no known use.

It seems quite apparent that UFO apparitions have been with us for a long time. It is reasonable to assume that many UFO sightings are labeled "UFO" simply because the observed object was too far away for proper identification—an unidentified, though terrestrial, flying object. There remains a significant number of reports that *cannot* be dismissed as hoaxes, weather phenomena, or misidentification of man-made objects. It is these reports that drive the skeptics crazy. It is humorous to see what lengths they will go to explain the sightings. Swamp gas, earthquake lights, weather balloons, or the planet Venus are the usual explanations given by avowed skeptics to disqualify sightings, the real identity of which they haven't the foggiest idea. It has become increasingly obvious that there are those whose agenda is focused upon debunking anything they cannot explain. I imagine that it pains these people greatly to even consider—much less reluctantly admit—the possibility of intelligent life elsewhere in our galaxy. I would love to know what the vocal skeptics admit privately. I think that, for whatever reasons, the most vocal skeptics have a need to ridicule people who believe in the reality of extraterrestrial visitations.

In response to the growing level of public interest and openness, the major media outlets such as NBC, The Discovery Channel, the Sci-Fi Channel, and others, have begun offering additional UFO-related content. From my own limited perspective, I have seen an increase in the frequency of requests for interviews from me. I also know that the people involved in SETI are all primed for making the Big Announcement when the signal that they know is out there finally comes in. They have not popped the champagne corks yet, but it is possible—even likely—that the bubbly could flow at any time, whether it be tomorrow or 20 years from now. Naturally, they have to be absolutely sure that the signal is genuine, but you can bet that there will be no holding back when it does come in. And I am sure that when the announcement is made, most people will accept it without reservation, rather than be overcome with the panic that the more paranoid among us would predict.

My own life and those of my family have been touched by the truth of otherworldly civilizations, and it is my hope that you, the reader, can feel that touch and look objectively, hopefully, and perhaps even lovingly upon the promise that future contact holds for humanity. Our job—indeed, our responsibility—is to provide future generations with truth, upon which they may make better decisions than the generations that preceded them. Our other job is to act responsibly when faced with evidence that the universe is big enough to be home to a great number of civilizations. As I've said before, to deny this would be to place human limits upon God's infinite capacity for creation.

The Vatican's chief astronomer and director of the Vatican Observatory, the Reverend Jose Funes, in a May 13, 2008 interview, stated that believing in aliens does not contradict faith in God. He said that the vastness of the universe means it is possible that there could be other life outside Earth—even intelligent life. He stated that such a notion "doesn't contradict our faith" because aliens could still be God's creatures. The interview was headlined "The extraterrestrial is my brother." Funes said that ruling out the existence of aliens would be like "putting limits" on God's creative freedom.

We are not alone!

EPILOGUE

UFO believers and skeptics alike have sometimes referred to the Roswell Incident as the biggest UFO story that almost wasn't. Those who are most cynical call it the biggest UFO non-event in history, or much ado about nothing. It's true that, for decades, no one talked much about the mysterious 1947 crash in the high desert of New Mexico, although, despite what many skeptics say, the silence didn't occur because Roswell was no big deal after all. Not to belabor the point, but there was a concerted effort to make the story go away...and it very nearly did. It was only due to the diligent work of ufologists such as Stanton Friedman, whose efforts have been both praised and damned, that the Roswell Incident reemerged into the public eye more than three decades after it happened. And now, for better or worse, the story has taken on a life of its own.

For my family, of course, the story never did go away. For the Marcels, Roswell has cut a swath both deep and wide, sweeping across generations and piercing the heart of our family in ways that went beyond the effects on my father's livelihood and reputation.

The legacy of Roswell reaches far beyond the Marcel family. Roswell is a story rich in political, sociological, scientific, historical, and even cosmological implications. Thousands of words have been written and spoken about Roswell; it is one of the most thoroughly examined incidents in UFO history. I don't expect that this one little book will do much to change anyone's mind about whether or not that long-ago crash in the desert was evidence of a visitation from a world beyond ours. The most I can do is tell my story and my father's, and I hope I have done an acceptable job of that.

As for changing anyone's mind, that's not my job. I am well aware that, as in most controversial matters, both sides have a significant stake in their opinions, and many aren't willing to seriously consider arguments from the other side. I'll grant that some UFO believers have been as guilty of this closed-mindedness as have skeptics. Some skeptics have even called *me* closed-minded, stubborn, foolish, or merely misguided for continuing to insist that the debris my father and I handled was "not of this world."

But I know what I saw and what I felt on that summer night in 1947. I know of my father's excitement, frustration, and ultimate despair as a result of Roswell. I know there is still more to this story than has yet been told. And I know that, although my experiences and observations do not prove beyond a skeptic's doubt that the Roswell crash came from an unearthly source, there is a lot of evidence supporting the "not of this world" school of thought. In any case, if sticking to my beliefs about Roswell is foolish or stubborn, then I proudly accept those mantles.

I don't know if we will ever know the entire truth about the Roswell Incident. According to the "official" story, the truth *was* revealed more than a dozen years ago, and we should all close the book on Roswell and turn our attention to something else. But to me, and to thousands of others all over the world, the concluding chapter has yet to be written. It might even be said that the Roswell Incident is but one volume in a very long series.

In the years since my father's death, I have shared as much of the Roswell story as I know. But as for the rest of the story, and the story beyond Roswell...those are not mine or yours to tell. Those are the stories for our children and our grandchildren. It is my deepest wish that their eyes, their minds, and their hearts will remain always open, so that they may experience a universe filled with wonders we can scarcely imagine.

APPENDIX
History of the 509th

Because the 509th Composite Bomb Group is so deeply associated with Roswell, I thought it would be appropriate to add a few words about them. In short, the 509th was an air combat wing organized for basically one purpose only: to engage in atomic bomb warfare against the Japanese empire during World War II. It was an elite wing composed of hand-picked officers.

Activated:	December 17, 1944
Country:	United States of America
Branch:	United States Army Air Forces
Type:	Composite bombardment group
Role:	Nuclear weapon bombardment
Size:	1767 personnel, 15 B-29 and 5 C-54 aircraft
Part of:	313th Bomb Wing, 20th Air Force
Garrison/HQ:	North Field, Tinian, Mariana Islands
Motto (1952):	Defensor Vindex (Defender Avenger)
Engagements:	Hiroshima, Nagasaki

The 509th was constituted December 9, 1944, and activated December 17, 1944, at Wendover Army Air Field, Utah, and commanded by Colonel Paul Tibbets. It was his job to organize a combat unit to deliver the atomic bombs to either German or Japanese targets. because the flying components consisted of both bomber and transport aircraft, the group was designated as a composite squadron. Colonel Tibbets had selected Wendover as the training site because of its remoteness and ease of keeping activities under cover. I recall my mother getting mail from my dad during this time of highly censored letters in which entire sentences were clipped from the onionskin paper they were written on.

On September 10, 1944, the 393rd Bomb Squadron, which was a B-29 unit, arrived at Wendover and was assigned directly to the Second Air Force until creation of the 509th Composite Bomb Group. Originally consisting of 21 crews, 15 were selected to continue training and were organized into three flights of five crews.

The 320th transport portion of the 509th became known as "The Green Hornet Line," and utilized C-46 and C-47 aircraft. B-29s, designated as "silverplate B-29s" in the combat wing of the 509th, had extensive modification to the bombay area with the installation of a weaponeer station. Reduction in the overall weight of the aircraft was also accomplished to offset the heavy loads they would be required to carry. A total of 14 silverplate B-29s were delivered to the 509th combat wing.

A rigorous candidate selection process was used to recruit personnel for the 509th, with an 80 percent washout rate. Those made a part of the unit were not allowed transfer until the end of the war, nor were they allowed to travel without escorts from Military Intelligence units. With the addition of the 1st Ordnance Squadron to its roster, the 509th Combined Group had an authorized strength of 225 officers and 1,542 enlisted men, almost all of whom were deployed to Tinian. The 320th TCS did not officially deploy to Tinian but kept its base of operations at Wendover.

The 509th began replacement of its 14 training silverplates in February of 1945 by transferring four to the 216th Base Unit. Each bombardier completed at least 50 practice drops of inert pumpkin bombs, and at that time Col. Tibbets declared his group combat-ready. On July 26, the USS *Indianapolis* delivered the components of Little Boy to Tinian. The 509th then delivered its deadly war-ending load to Hiroshima and Nagasaki. Hiroshima was devastated by Little Boy, the uranium bomb, on August 6, 1945, and Nagasaki was devastated by Fat Man on August 9, 1945. The instruments of Japanese surrender were signed on the battleship *Missouri BB 63* on the morning of September 2, 1945.

Post-War History

In November 1945 the 509th Composite Bomb Group was relocated to Roswell Army Air Field, and the eight silverplate bombers that had been delivered to Wendover in August also joined the group. Colonel Blanchard replaced Colonel Tibbets as the group commander on January 22 of 1946, and also became the first commander of the 509th Bomb Wing.

The group was assigned to Strategic Air Command in March of 1946, one of 11 units. At the time SAC was formed, the 509th was the only unit that had experience with nuclear weapons. In April of 1946, the 509th took part in Operation Crossroads, which was a series of two atomic bomb tests at Bikini at Kwajalein islands. One was an over-water explosion, the Able test, and one was a subsurface explosion, the Baker test.

In July of 1946, the group was renamed the 509th Bombardment Group as the transportation portion of the 509th was disbanded, and in November of 1947 the group became the combat component of the 509th, operational in September of 1948. The 27 operational silverplate B-29s were transferred in 1949 to the 97th Bomb Wing at Briggs Air Force Base, El Paso, when the group converted to B-50 Superfortresses. The 509th was deactivated June 16, 1952. The group was redesignated 509th Operations Group in March of 1993, and activated as the flying component of the 509th Bomb Wing for B-2 stealth bombers at Whiteman Air Force Base in Missouri. The 509th is equipped with all 20 of the USAF's B-2 Spirit bombers.

INDEX

A

Able test, 39-40

Abrams, Viaud Aleen, 29, 120, 133-134

Alcubierre drive, 146-147

Aldebaran, 150

alien bodies, 13, 61, 73-74, 163

Allen, Oscar Kelly, 29

Almogordo, 48

AM and JC DuPont General
     Store, 29

American Radio Relay League, 30

Antartica, 155

Apollo 14, 157

Arabela, New Mexico, 83

Arecibo Telescope, 160

Army Air Force Intelligence
     School, 31, 35

Arnold, Kenneth, 13, 47

Aurora, Texas, 162-163

B

Bakelite, 53, 59, 92

Baker test, 39-40

balsa wood, 90-91

Barnett, Grady, 13

Berliner, Don, 12

Berlitz, Charles, 12, 14

Bikini Atoll, 39

black government, 100-103

Blanchard, William, 12-14, 16,
     40, 50, 60, 65, 72

Bock's Car, 37

box kite, 81, 86

Brazel, Bill, 59

Brazel, William Mac, 16, 20, 49-
     50, 59, 81-82

Bruno, Giordano, 158

C

Capitol Building, 97-98, 123

Carlson, Eric, 107-108

Cavitt, Sheridan, 12, 16, 20, 50-51

Chernovshev, Igor, 112

CIA 121

Cold War, 77-79

Contact, 160

Corona, New Mexico, 49-50

Crash at Corona, 12

Crawford, Don, 108

Creator, 153-154

D

debris, 22, 52-61, 65, 69, 101
    field, 49, 51, 61, 82
    fine strands, 59
    foil, 53-54
    lack of electric, 53, 55
    metal beams, 53, *see also* I-beams
    plastic, 53, 56, 59
debunkers, 15-16, 22
Department of Defense, 40
Drake, Frank, 150
Dubose, Thomas Jefferson, 16
Dutton, William, 111

E

earthquake lights, 163
electromagnetic pulse, 111
electronic components, 53, 55, 91 *see also* debris
Enola Gay, 37
extraterrestrial life, 22-23, 59, 103, 153-165
    public reaction to, 102, 152

F

false vacuum, 148
Fat Man, 37
Figel, Walt, 107-108
509th Composite Bomb Group, 16, 35, 171-174
flying disc, *see* flying saucer
flying disc statement, 64-65
Flying Saucer Review, 14
flying saucers, 12-13, 17, 47-48, 61
foil, 20, 53-54, *see also* debris
Fort Worth Army Air Base, 20, 60, 65, 72
Foster Ranch, 20, 49-50, 60, 73
Freedom of Information Act, 112, 152-153
Friedman, Stanton, 11-17, 21, 168
Funes, Jose, 164-165

G

Golden Globe Awards, 123
Goldwater, Barry, 99, 102

H

ham radio, 12, 16, 30
Hans-Adam II, 97-98, 122
Harrisburg, Pennsylvania, 31
Haut, Walter, 16
Henderson, Pappy, 73
Hiroshima, 16, 37
Holter, Jeff, 40
Hopkins, Budd, 161
Houma, Louisiana, 12, 15-16,
    28, 120
Houston, Texas, 30
Hubble Space Telescope, 154

I

I-beam, 56-58, 99
    symbols on, 57-59, 88-89
Independence Day, 161
Intercontinental Ballistic Missiles
    (ICBM), 107-108, 111
interstellar travel, 25, 103, 106,
    144-150
Iraq, 15, 22, 123

J

Japanese Instrument of Surrender, 38
Japanese spies, 31
Jennings, Peter, 15
Johnson, James Bond, 65

K

Kaminski, Robert, 111
Kenneth Arnold sighting, 13, 47

L

Little Boy, 37

M

Majestic, 99
Malmstrom Air Force Base, 107
Marcel, Adelaide, 28
Marcel family, 28-35, 129-142, 168

Marcel, Jesse, Jr., 15, 17, 26,
        118, 120-123
    childhood play of, 46-47
    and debris, 52-61
    meeting with government
        official, 97-101
    mysterious phone calls
        to, 96, 100, 123
    promise to father, 25
    reasons for writing, 22
    service in Iraq, 15, 22, 123
    visit to Brazil, 125-126
Marcel, Jesse, Sr., 11-13, 15-16,
        19-20, 26, 119, 120
    alcohol dependency of, 133
    awards given to, 42-43
    behavior after Roswell
        Incident, 132-135
    behavior prior to Roswell
        Incident, 130-132
    character attacks on, 22
    and debris, 50-61
    dedication to military, 42
    disillusionment with the
        military, 132-135
    ham radio use by, 16, 30

interest in radio, 29-30, 131
and military, 23
military silencing of, 51
military training of, 31,
        35, 39-40
photograph of, 21
reputation of, 24
Marcel, Linda, 85, 96, 116-127,
        130, 136-137
Marcel, Theodule, 28
Mars, 155-156
Meiwald, Fred, 110
methane, 155
missiles, 75, 109-111
Mitchell, Edgar, 157
ML-307 reflector, 38, 89
Mogul balloons, 38-39, 55-56,
        60, 64-65, 70, 72-73, 76,
        78-83, 90-92
    balsa wood used in, 86,
        90-91
    electric components of, 91
    paper used in, 90
    tape on, 87-90
Mogul device, *see* Mogul balloon

Montana National Guard, 95

Moore, Charles, 79, 82, 86-92

Moore, William L., 12-14, 16

Mount Baker, 47

Mount Rainier, 47

Muir, 125

Mutual UFO Network
	(MUFON), 14, 121

Mystery Stalks The Prairie, 112

N

Nagasaki, 16, 37

nanobe, 156

National Aeronautics and Space
	Administration (NASA),
		121, 145, 148, 152

Nasca Plains, 162

nuclear accident, 75

O

Occam's razor, 156

Officers' Club, 40, 133

Operation Crossroads, 39

Oscar Flight Control Center, 109

P

paper, 90

Pearl Harbor, 31

Philippines, 35

Pioneer 10, 149

plastic, 53, 56, 59 *see also* debris

Project Bluebook, 152

Project Grudge, 152

Project Mogul, 78, 86, 89
	Flight #11, 82-83
	Flight #4, 72, 81-82
	Flight #10, 81, 83

R

radar targets, 54, 64, 68-69, 72, 92
	Rawin, 38-39, 68, 80,
		82, 86, 89, 91

radio, 29-30, 131
	transmitter, 56, 80

radiosonde, 56, 80

Raiders of the Lost Ark, 100

Ramjet, 149

Ramy, Roger, 20, 60, 65, 68-69

Randle, Kevin D., 123

Regan, Ronald, 153

Roman Catholic Church, 158

Roswell, 123, 137-138

Roswell, Legacy, The, 26

Roswell, New Mexico, 12, 16, 19

Roswell Army Air Field (RAAF),
    20, 39, 50

Roswell Incident, 11, 19, 25,
    123, 141, 167
        effects on Marcel family,
            129-142
        fiftieth anniversary of,
            124, 138
        and Jesse Marcel, Sr., 23,
            28, 41, 43
        official government
            explanation of,
            21, 64-76, 169

Roswell Incident, The, 12, 14

Roswell Report: Case Closed, The,
    55, 64, 74-76, 93

*Roswell Report: Fact vs. Fiction in
    the New Mexico Desert,
    The*, 17

rubber, 20

Russian government, 121-122

S

Sagan, Carl, 150, 160

Salas, Robert, 109-110

Sasquatch, 116

Schmitt, Donald R., 123

Search for Extraterrestrial
    Intelligence (SETI), 16,
    158-159, 164

Senate Appropriations
    Committee, 100

Shandera, Jaime, 14

Shell Oil Company, 30

Socorro, New Mexico, 86

sonobuoy, 80, 82

Sputnik, 116-117

Star Trek, 106

Strategic Air Command (SAC),
    50, 112

Strieber, Whitley, 99
summer of 1947, 13, 27, 40
swamp gas, 152, 163
symbols, 57-59, 88-89, 99, *see also*
    I-beam

T

tape, 87-90
telegram, 69-70
tinfoil hats, 22, 101, 121
Tinian, 36

U

UFO Cover-up? Live, 14, 121
UFO Crash at Roswell, 123
UFO Magazine, 15
UFOs ARE Real, 14-15
unexplained UFO events, 106-113
Unites States government, 24-25,
    151-153

Unsolved Mysteries, 15
uranium bomb, 37

V

Variable Specific Impulse
    Magnetoplasma Rocket
    (VASIMR), 147-148
Vatican Observatory, 164
Venus, 163

W

weather ballon, 21, 63, 65, 68-
    70, 74, 82, 163
    envelope, 68
Weaver, Richard, 17
White Sands, 48
Wolverton, Keith, 112
Wright-Patterson Air Force Base,
    73, 99, 102

Y

Yeager, Don, 40

Z

zero-point energy, 148

ABOUT THE AUTHORS

Jesse Marcel, Jr.

Born August 30, 1936, in Houston, Texas, Marcel is a retired military officer who served as a medical officer in the United States Navy from 1962 to 1971, having received his specialty training in

Otolaryngology while in the Navy. He joined the Navy in 1962 just in time to take part in the Cuban Missile Crisis by serving onboard a troop transport ship, just missing being part of the invasion of Cuba when the crisis was peacefully concluded. Marcel opened his medical practice in Helena, Montana, in 1971, and eventually joined the Montana National Guard as a medical officer in 1975, earning his flight surgeon wings at Ft. Rucker, Alabama. In those days the flight surgeons were allowed to solo in helicopters.

During his career in the National Guard, he was appointed State Surgeon of the State of Montana, and retired from the military a second time on his 60th birthday in 1996. The Iraqi war (Operation Iraqi Freedom) required his return to the military in September of 2004, and he spent the next 13 months as a flight surgeon for the 189th Helicopter Battalion in Iraq. He spent his 69th birthday there, and eventually flew more than 225 combat hours in a Blackhawk helicopter. Currently he is employed by the VA Hospital at Ft. Harrison, Montana, but is in the process of retiring. He and his wife, Linda, live outside Helena and look forward to slowing down and enjoying life.

More than 40 major media outlets have interviewed Jesse, including Fox News, *Larry King Live*, Channel 9 from Australia, Fox's Sean Hannity, Smithsonian Television, NBC's *Today Show*, CBC Radio, Jeff Rense, *Coast to Coast*, and the National Geographic Channel.

Jesse Marcel, Jr., standing next to a Blackhawk Helicopter in a landing zone just outside of Baghdad, summer 2005.

Linda Marcel

Born in Montana on July 29, 1951, of a veterinarian/cowboy and a dedicated nurse, Linda's grandparents were Montana homesteaders with roots in Russia and Germany.

At this time she is a semi-retired nurse, mother of five, and grandmother of 10, so she keeps quite busy entertaining her grandchildren as well as maintaining her flower garden and taking care of a 4H club.

She has seen the Northern Lights and *Sputnik* (and was terrified of it), but has never seen a genuine UFO, although she believes in life elsewhere, as well as the awesome possibility of it having visited us.

Other Paranormal Titles from NEW PAGE BOOKS

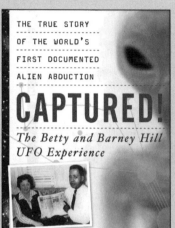

CAPTURED! THE BETTY AND BARNEY HILL UFO EXPERIENCE

The True Story of the World's First Documented Alien Abduction

EAN 978-1-56414-971-8 $16.99

"The famous 1961 Betty and Barney Hill abduction by non-humans is taken apart, meticulously re-examined by Betty's niece and nuclear physicist Stanton T. Friedman, and reinforced by the pressure of facts."

—Linda Moulton Howe, Emmy Award-winning TV producer, reporter, and

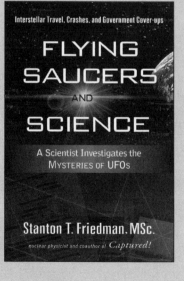

FLYING SAUCERS AND SCIENCE

A Scientist Investigates the Mysteries of UFOs, Interstellar Travel, Crashes, and Government Cover-Ups

EAN 978-1-60163-011-7 $16.99

"Friedman, having worked in top secret government rocket programs, is able to establish the truth about UFO secrecy and how it works. He has established a new norm for scientific inquiry in the UFO field."

—John F. Schuessler, Mutual UFO Network, Inc., international director emeritus

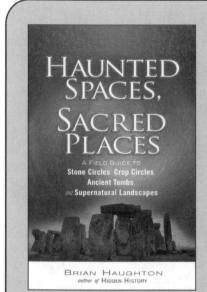
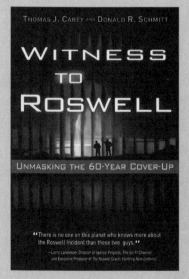